A Sea of Red

50 Years with the Chiefs & The Kansas City Star

» Priest Holmes leaps for a score.

>> *Pete Stoyanovich slips during the famous "Rain Game" in 1998.*

A Sea of Red

50 Years with the Chiefs and The Kansas City Star
by Jeffrey Flanagan
and The Kansas City Star

Author: Jeffrey Flanagan
Contributions: The Kansas City Star
Editor: Doug Weaver
Copy Editor: Les Weatherford
Design: Kelly Ludwig, Ludwig Design
Photography: The Kansas City Star, Hank Young Photography, Sports Illustrated, Janet Rogers Photography
Production assistance: Jo Ann Groves

Published by Kansas City Star Books
1729 Grand Blvd.
Kansas City, Mo. 64108
All rights reserved.

Copyright © 2009 by The Kansas City Star Co.

No part of this book may be reproduced, stored in a retrieval system, or transmitted in any form or by any means electronic, mechanical, photocopying, recording or otherwise, without the prior consent of the publisher. Permission is granted to make copies of the patterns pages only for your own private, personal use, not for commercial use.

First edition, first printing
ISBN: 978-1-933466-94-1
Library of Congress Control Number: 2009935613
Printed in the United States.

To order copies, call StarInfo at 816-234-4636 and say "operator."
www.TheKansasCityStore.com

Dedication

I'd like to dedicate this book to my mom, Luanne Grignon, who has been simply the greatest supporter a son could ever want.

About the author

Jeffrey Flanagan was a sportswriter and sports columnist at The Kansas City Star for 19 years. He also was a sportswriter for the Portsmouth (N.H.) Herald, the Decatur (Ill.) Herald & Review and The Arizona Republic.

He has written two previous books: *Lau's Laws on Hitting* and *The Shame of Me*, the story of Royals broadcaster Ryan Lefebvre's struggle with depression.

Flanagan lives in Kansas City, Mo., on the Country Club Plaza.

» Dwayne Bowe

Table of Contents

Foreword 6
Introduction 8

Part I
The Glory Years 1960-1970

Chapter 1   The Foolish Club... 10
Chapter 2   Dallas to Kansas City.. 15
Chapter 3   A Powerhouse Team 19
Chapter 4   The AFL Title and Super Bowl I................................. 31
Chapter 5   The Road to Super Bowl IV... 43

Part II
A Team Adrift 1971-1988

Chapter 6   The Game That Changed a Franchise 57
Chapter 7   The End of the Hank Stram Era............................. 64
Chapter 8   Marv Levy and the Wing-T 74

Part III
A Team for Kansas City 1989-2009

Chapter 9   Peterson-Schottenheimer
                  Era Restores Hope 94
Chapter 10   Greatness Arrives... 111
Chapter 11   The Marty-Carl Breakup.. 133
Chapter 12   The End of the Carl Regime 164

Foreword by Len Dawson

It's hard to believe we're now celebrating 50 years of this franchise.

I don't think any of us can truly understand the magnitude of Lamar Hunt's decision to first have a dream such as the American Football League, and then to create a team like the Dallas Texans and bring them eventually here to Kansas City.

Lamar and the Chiefs have affected so many lives. It is truly remarkable. I know I wouldn't be in Kansas City. I wouldn't have played in Super Bowls. I wouldn't be in the Hall of Fame. I wouldn't be a broadcaster. But I'm just one of so many people that Lamar touched throughout his life. He was such a great innovator, from the AFL to the naming of the Super Bowl to finally getting the NFL to accept the two-point conversion, which was an old AFL toy. And he never stopped helping people.

People have often asked me what Kansas City would be like without the Chiefs. I can't even imagine it. They have become such a part of the community since the 1960s. They are a big part of people's lives here.

Rooting for the Chiefs bonds people. And as with any franchise or business, there is a need to reach out to the people. That's where The Kansas City Star has played a big role throughout the years. When the Chiefs came to Kansas City, there wasn't the big media and the Internet that we have now. But The Star was there every day, home or away, covering the team and getting word out to the masses – not just in Kansas City but also in the entire region. There has always been a relationship between the Chiefs and The Star. I know that the players may not have always agreed with what was written about them or the team, but they always read it.

To me, the Chiefs are a very unique organization founded by a very unique man in Lamar Hunt. It is my pleasure to honor them in this book.

Len Dawson

Introduction
A Sea of Red

It's easy to forget how it all started. It's easy to forget the bizarre chain of events that led to the creation of the American Football League and then ultimately to a team called the Kansas City Chiefs.

Today, no other sports team and no other business impacts Kansas City quite like the Chiefs. For home games on fall Sundays, Arrowhead Stadium is packed with fervent Chiefs fans. Hours before the game, the parking lots overflow with tailgate parties. Smoke from barbecues fills the sky over Arrowhead and can be seen for miles. Yes, on any given fall Sunday, a Chiefs game is truly *the* event in Kansas City.

In 2009, we celebrate the 50th season of the Chiefs franchise. And since the franchise's arrival in Kansas City in 1963, The Kansas City Star has been there to cover it all, taking fans through every Chiefs moment, good and bad.

A Sea of Red takes you through the journey of the team's inception in Dallas, its move to Kansas City and all the significant developments in team history, as reported on a daily basis by The Kansas City Star.

Today's fans perhaps have only passing knowledge of how the Chiefs came to be. Obviously, they know enough to give thanks to Lamar Hunt, the team's founder. But do fans realize they should also thank legendary Chicago Bears owner George Halas? After all, if Halas hadn't been so determined to prevent Hunt from bringing an NFL expansion team to Dallas in 1959, Hunt never would have spawned the idea for an AFL. And, of course, there never would have been the Kansas City Chiefs.

It was only after the NFL had spurned Hunt's attempts to land a team – Hunt also unsuccessfully pursued the NFL's Chicago Cardinals – that he dreamed up the idea of a competing league and ultimately sold that notion to seven other owners, all of whom became famously known as The Foolish Club.

A Sea of Red takes you through it all – the Super Bowls, the hirings, the firings, the down years, the rebirth of the organization, the wild ride in the 1990s when Arrowhead came to life again, the stunning acquisitions of Joe Montana and Marcus Allen, the high-flying Dick Vermeil years – all seen through the watchful lens of The Kansas City Star.

All photographs in *A Sea of Red* were taken by Kansas City Star photographers unless otherwise noted. Hank Young Photography contributed to the cover.

» *Trent Green led a potent offense under Dick Vermeil.*

Part 1: The Glory Years 1960-1970

Chapter 1

The Foolish Club

Lamar Hunt, who was born in El Dorado, Ark., inherited a fortune from his father, whose wealth had its foundation in the oil business. But Lamar's passion as a child was sports. Any sport. In fact, his childhood nickname was "Games." But while his friends were obsessed with box scores and player statistics and such, Lamar always seemed more fascinated with another number – attendance.

"I always was amazed at the number of paying customers to events," Hunt said. "I always admired the events or the sports that drew people."

Hunt tried sports himself. He was a backup tight end on the Southern Methodist University football team. But he knew his calling was as an entrepreneur. His first business venture after college was batting cages. And then miniature golf.

"Whatever skill I had at the time was probably my ability to sell tickets," he said.

But Hunt's vision changed forever on Dec. 28, 1958. That's the day

» *Lamar Hunt, far right, poses with the seven other members of The Foolish Club.*

"Games" sat in front of a black-and-white television set and watched perhaps the greatest game ever played – the NFL title game between the league's glamour team, the New York Giants, and the Baltimore Colts, led by Johnny Unitas, at Yankee Stadium.

Hunt suddenly knew his destiny – pro football.

> *"It was that game," said Jack Steadman, former Chiefs chairman. "When Lamar saw that game, he said: 'The NFL cannot fail. Pro football cannot fail. This is the beginning of it, and I want to get in on the beginning of it.'"*

Hunt, of course, knew pro football had been around for decades. But baseball dominated the American landscape at the time. Horse racing drew bigger crowds than pro football. But Hunt knew right then that television and pro football would become one of the greatest marriages in American history.

The problem, of course, was getting into the exclusive NFL owners club. Hunt wanted to buy the struggling Chicago Cardinals in 1959 and relocate them to his hometown in Dallas. The NFL rebuffed him every time. Hunt sought an expansion team for Dallas. Halas said no way.

"All Halas had to do was give Lamar a franchise in Dallas," said Buffalo Bills owner Ralph Wilson, an original member of The Foolish Club. "If he had, there never would have been an AFL."

And there might never have been the Kansas City Chiefs. Or an Arrowhead Stadium. Or the Super Bowl, for that matter. Think about that.

After Hunt was turned down for the final time at the NFL's February meetings in 1959, he came up with a plan on a flight back to Dallas. He jotted down notes for a new league to compete with the NFL. America was falling in love with pro football, and Hunt reasoned that there would be plenty of interest in a new league.

Eventually, Hunt talked seven other owners into throwing in $25,000 each to form an eight-team league. In August of 1959, Hunt made the announcement: The AFL was born. And Hunt would own the Dallas Texans.

"I always thought the name 'American Football League' was part of its appeal," Hunt said. "In baseball, there had been an American League and a National League. That was comfortable for the fans. It had been that way for 60 years. Those leagues played in the World Series, the biggest sporting event at the time.

» *Norma and Lamar on their wedding day.*

» *Lamar was determined to make the AFL a success.*

"We already had a National Football League, so it seemed natural to have an American Football League. People could immediately visualize the concept."

It didn't take long for the NFL to visualize the concept, or the potential for competition. Within weeks, the NFL announced that it was expanding and that one of those expansion teams would be in Dallas.

That's when the NFL came back to Hunt. While the NFL had offered its Dallas expansion team to Texas businessman Clint Murchison, it was Murchison who offered Hunt a part of the team. Hunt said no. Murchison then offered to step down and give Hunt the entire operation. This was Hunt's chance to get what he originally wanted – an owner's seat in the NFL.

Hunt said no again.

"It wasn't a difficult decision," Hunt said. "I had invested a lot of emotion and time and energy into the concept of the AFL. I felt I owed it to myself and the fellow AFL owners to stick with it."

The AFL started play in 1960, and Hunt's Texans were beaten 21-20 by the Chargers in Los Angeles. The team finished 8-6 and in second place in the AFL's Western Division. But more important to Hunt, his league was off and running.

While the league wasn't exactly a financial hit, observers at the time seemed certain the league would make it. Count former Raiders coach and longtime announcer John Madden among them.

> **"When I knew the AFL was going to make it was after that first year,"** Madden said, **"Someone went up to Lamar's dad, H.L Hunt, and said, 'Your son, with this new league, has lost $1 million' and Lamar's dad just said, 'Well, at that rate, he can only go another 100 years.'**

"That statement by Lamar's dad said this AFL isn't going to go away. That's when the NFL realized it, too."

Chapter 2

Dallas to Kansas City

Lamar Hunt may have known, too, that the AFL was going to stick around. But Hunt also knew that Dallas wasn't big enough for both the NFL's Cowboys or Hunt's Texans. Both teams suffered poor attendance. It was Hunt who looked for greener pastures.

Despite the fact that the Texans won the AFL championship in 1962, Hunt began scoping other cities. He did so with a rather unscientific approach. There were no market research studies. Hunt relied on the convenience of geography. First, he set his sights on New Orleans, just 447 air miles from Dallas. A short flight from his home, he reasoned.

Chiefs fans may never know how closely they came to losing their beloved team to the city of New Orleans. But fortunately for Kansas City, Hunt couldn't secure a lease agreement with Tulane Stadium. Next stop, Kansas City.

Mayor H. Roe "Chief" Bartle actually had been courting Hunt since the Texans won the 1962 AFL title. Hunt admittedly was intrigued by Kansas City but didn't know all that much about it.

"That might have been a naive way to look at things," Hunt said of the process. "Kansas City was very much a baseball town then, and that stands to reason because they had a major-league team. They didn't have a pro football team, and they didn't have any college teams that played right in Kansas City. But I did understand that there was a potential of a six-state area to draw fans from."

Hunt and Bartle met as secretly as possible in those days. Hunt registered at downtown hotels under the name "Mr. Lamar." Bartle even introduced him around town as "Mr. Lamar."

Hunt's right-hand man, Jack Steadman, performed much of the covert operation when Hunt was back in Dallas. While Hunt was introduced by Bartle around town as "Mr. Lamar," Steadman was known as "Jack X," an out-of-town IRS agent working on a secret project.

"The whole thing was so hush-hush," Steadman said. "In fact, my office

» Above: Lamar Hunt forever changed Kansas City by moving his Texans here.

» Left: The Chiefettes: The early version of the Chiefs cheerleaders.

The Glory Years 1960-1970 | 15

in Dallas didn't even know where I was."

Hunt, Steadman and Bartle eventually ironed out a deal for the Texans to play in Municipal Stadium. Naturally, the name "Texans" needed to be changed, and "Chiefs" was chosen, partly out of respect for Bartle and partly out of respect for the area's Native American heritage.

Hunt envisioned a team that would be supported regionally. The team's first logo depicted an American Indian running across the outline of Missouri, Kansas, Iowa, Nebraska, Oklahoma and Arkansas.

The Kansas City Chiefs officially were born.

> *"Lamar saved our town," said longtime Chiefs broadcaster Bill Grigsby. "First, when he came in, everyone wondered what this new league was. Then, in three years, they showed us what it was.*
>
> *"It changed the personality of the town. It's the single biggest thing that ever happened for him to bring the team here. We didn't know it at the time. We didn't realize this team would get in the National Football League."*

The Chiefs' 1963 draft class included defensive tackle Buck Buchanan, linebacker Bobby Bell and guard Ed Budde. Expectations were high for pro football in Kansas City.

But for the team's first preseason game in 1963, only 5,721 fans showed up at Municipal Stadium. Worse yet, the season-ticket goal of 25,000 fell about 10,000 short.

The Chiefs didn't perform much better on the field, going 5-7-2 and 7-7 in their first two seasons in Kansas City. The season-ticket base dropped to under 10,000.

But after a 7-5-2 season in 1965, the Redcoaters were spawned. The Redcoaters – a group of civic leaders and businessmen – served as voluntary season-ticket salespeople, a tradition that carries on today. Season-ticket sales immediately jumped to 22,000 for the 1966 season, when Kansas City claimed its first AFL title.

Indeed, the Chiefs were here to stay.

Courtesy of Hank Young Photography

Chiefs' Logo Stands the Test of Time

Several NFL teams have felt the urge to alter their logo and helmets through the years, teams such as the Patriots, the Bills and the Broncos.

The Chiefs have always resisted that urge.

"I guess I was always a stickler on how the logos and the uniforms looked," Chiefs founder Lamar Hunt once said. "I never thought it really needed to be changed."

When Hunt moved the Dallas Texans to Kansas City in 1963, naturally he needed a new logo for the Chiefs' helmet to replace the Texas silhouette.

So, Hunt sat down one day with a 5-cent pencil, a legal pad and some ideas.

The logo that Hunt settled on eventually became one of the most classic and powerful icons in the NFL, according to one league executive.

One image that Hunt scribbled on his legal pad was an arrowhead with interlocking initials "KC." That's the image that stuck with him.

"I was scratching around on the pad," Hunt said. "I got a picture of the 49ers helmet -- they had those interlocking letters, and I thought that was very attractive. A lot of baseball teams have that interlocking letter design."

These days, of course, any such logo design would invite a huge undertaking led by design firms and market researchers. That was hardly the case with Hunt and the Chiefs' logo.

"I drew it up, and I liked it," he said. "I am sure I showed it to Jack Steadman and Hank (Stram). But we didn't do anything more than that. Now, teams do surveys of public opinion and get all this input and what would look good and what they should do.

"If we had done all those things back then, the AFL would have never been started."

The Chiefs' helmet logo also played another key role in the history of the Chiefs and Kansas City: Hunt believed the distinctive nature of the logo helped persuade influential figures to name the stadium at the Truman Sports Complex "Arrowhead Stadium."

"Had we not had that emblem on our helmet, Arrowhead Stadium probably would have been named something else," Hunt said. "We were looking for something distinctive to set it apart from other stadiums, and I think the logo is what did it."

Chapter 3
A Powerhouse Team

The Chiefs' 1966 season changed everything. Kansas Citians began to truly embrace the team, and fans who poured into Municipal Stadium became enamored of the Chiefs' potent offense.

The architect behind that high-powered offense was head coach Hank Stram, who brought many innovations to pro football, most notably the moving pocket, which allowed quarterback Len Dawson to avoid rushes, survey the field better and create unique angles for passing lanes.

Stram was born in 1923 in Chicago and grew up in Gary, Ind. His father was a Polish-born professional wrestler named Henry Wilszek, who also performed in the Barnum & Bailey circus. It was the circus that changed Henry's last name to Stram.

Although his parents didn't want Hank to play sports, he excelled in football, baseball and basketball in high school and earned a scholarship to Purdue in 1941. He enlisted in the Army Reserve in 1943 and remained in the service for three years. He returned to Purdue in 1946 and lettered in football and baseball.

Stram graduated in 1948 and spent the next 12 years as an assistant football coach at Purdue, SMU, Notre Dame and Miami. It was Stram's reputation as an innovator that caught Hunt's attention – Hunt envisioned the AFL as an alternative league that would feature wide-open offenses.

"It was his personality and the fact that he wanted the job," Hunt said. "It was very apparent that he wanted to be a head coach. He had a very good reputation as far as offensive football. He was a good teacher. He knew how to describe things and articulate what he wanted."

Offense was never an issue during the franchise's early years. During the Texans' 1962 championship season, Dawson ran Stram's offense to perfection and threw for 2,759 yards and 29 touchdowns – gaudy numbers for the era.

"He knew how to win," Dawson said of Stram. "A lot of people thought

» *Mike Garrett, left, fueled the running game.*

The Glory Years 1960-1970 | 19

Courtesy of Hank Young Photography

we always had the best talent, but that wasn't always the case. He knew how to take advantage of our strength and the other team's weaknesses."

But make no mistake: The Chiefs did have plenty of offensive talent.

In 1966, the Chiefs had a solid offensive line led by left guard Ed Budde and left tackle Jim Tyrer. Dawson had imposing targets to throw to, such as wide receiver Otis Taylor and tight end Fred Arbanas. And Dawson had a solid backfield with running backs Mike Garrett and Curtis McClinton.

The Chiefs were loaded defensively, too. The defensive line featured Jerry Mays, Ed Lothamer, Chuck Hurston and Buck Buchanan. The linebackers were Bobby Bell, Sherrill Headrick and E.J. Holub. In the secondary: Fred "The Hammer" Williamson, Willie Mitchell, Bobby Hunt and Johnny Robinson.

The Chiefs also had the best punter in the game in Jerrel Wilson.

"We were a confident group, too," Dawson said.

The Chiefs rolled through the preseason that year, winning all four games. And they started the regular season by pounding Buffalo, Oakland and Boston, all on the road. The Chiefs averaged nearly 40 points a game.

"There wasn't much we couldn't do offensively," Dawson said.

The biggest crowd in the Chiefs' brief history – 43,885 – packed into Municipal Stadium on Oct. 2 and greeted the unbeaten Chiefs, who promptly fell 29-14 to Buffalo. But it was one of only two losses during the regular season, and it was clear that as home attendance reached an average of nearly 40,000, Kansas City had truly adopted the Chiefs.

"I think everyone could feel that we were becoming a big deal in the city," Dawson said. "We could feel the support."

Courtesy of Hank Young Photography

≫ *By the mid-1960s, Len Dawson had plenty of offensive weapons from which to choose.*

As the Chiefs rolled to an 11-2-1 season, they prepared for a Jan. 1 showdown at Buffalo for the AFL title.

There was also a special prize for the victor – a meeting with the champions of the NFL to declare the champion of pro football.

The merger

Before the 1966 season, owners in both the AFL and the NFL realized that a continuing war between the leagues would be destructive on both sides. Bidding wars to sign college draft choices had gotten out of hand, and it became clear that only the richest teams in either league could win these bidding wars.

Something had to be done.

Tex Schramm, Dallas Cowboys president, made the initial move, setting up a secret meeting in April of 1996 with Hunt in a parking lot outside of the Dallas airport, Love Field. That 30-minute discussion marked the beginning of AFL-NFL merger talks, a merger that would forever change the landscape of professional sports in America.

By June, the two leagues announced the merger, a deal that would include a championship game between the leagues that would start after the 1966 season. Of course, as anyone from Kansas City would know, that game would become known as the Super Bowl – named by Hunt after he had watched his daughter play with a popular toy called a Super Ball at the time.

» *Fred Williamson was one of the early flamboyant stars of professional football.*

The completed merger also called for the end of the American Football League by 1970. The two leagues would become one, with the Browns, the Steelers and the Colts switching to the newly formed American Football Conference by 1970 and thus forming two 13-team conferences.

Courtesy of Hank Young Photography

>> *Dawson and Hank Stram always worked to stay on the same page.*

Buck Buchanan

Bobby Bell: The Greatest Chief Ever?

The Kansas City Star
Feb. 2, 1983

On Monday, Chiefs linebacker Bobby Bell learned he had become the first Chiefs player to be elected to the Pro Football Hall of Fame in Canton, Ohio.

"It was a total surprise," Bell said. "It's like you fantasize about something. I never dreamed that would happen to me. You know how you get butterflies inside? That's how I feel."

Bell may have been surprised, but anyone who played with or against Bell wasn't. Many observers consider Bell perhaps the greatest Chiefs player of all time.

"If you were to make a highlight reel of how to make an open-field tackle," former coach Hank Stram said, "he'd be the guy you'd use as a model."

Bell had been a high school quarterback and then, briefly, a running back at the University of Minnesota. Then he became a defensive end at Minnesota before his pro career at linebacker. He was also the deep snapper on punts and place kicks.

Bell was known as a playmaker. He returned six interceptions for touchdowns and once grabbed an onside kick and raced 53 yards for a touchdown.

"I've never been associated with another player, or seen another player, who I thought could play any position and help you win like Bobby Bell could," Stram said.

Beginning in 1966, Bell made six straight all-AFL and all-AFC teams. He was also All-Pro (NFL) in 1970 and 1971 and played in the first two Pro Bowls.

Yet what Stram appreciated the most about Bell was his attitude.

"I'd be on the field," Stram said, "and I'd holler to Bobby, and he might be all the way down at the other end of the field. He'd stop what he was doing, just pick up his helmet and run to right where you were and wonder what you wanted. Attitude wise, he was a rookie in all the years we had him. I think if you had a team full of Bobby Bells, you'd want to coach forever, and you'd win forever."

Courtesy of Hank Young Photography

» The Chiefs were an innovative team – as evidenced by their two-row huddle – with an innovative coaching staff. To the right, Mike Garrett powers into the end zone as the Chiefs whip Buffalo in the AFL title game in 1967.

The Glory Years 1960-1970 | 27

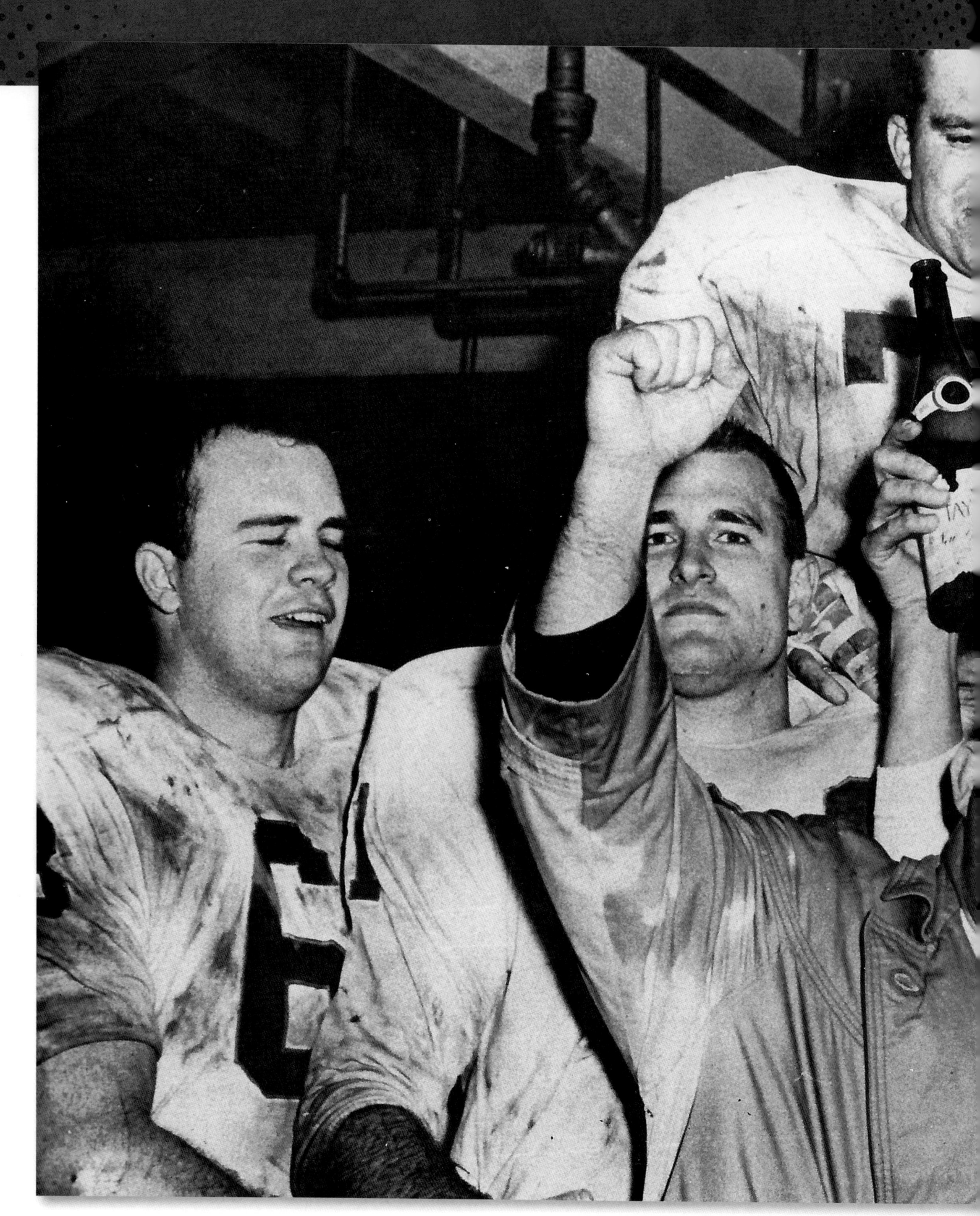

28 | A Sea of Red

The Glory Years 1960-1970 | 29

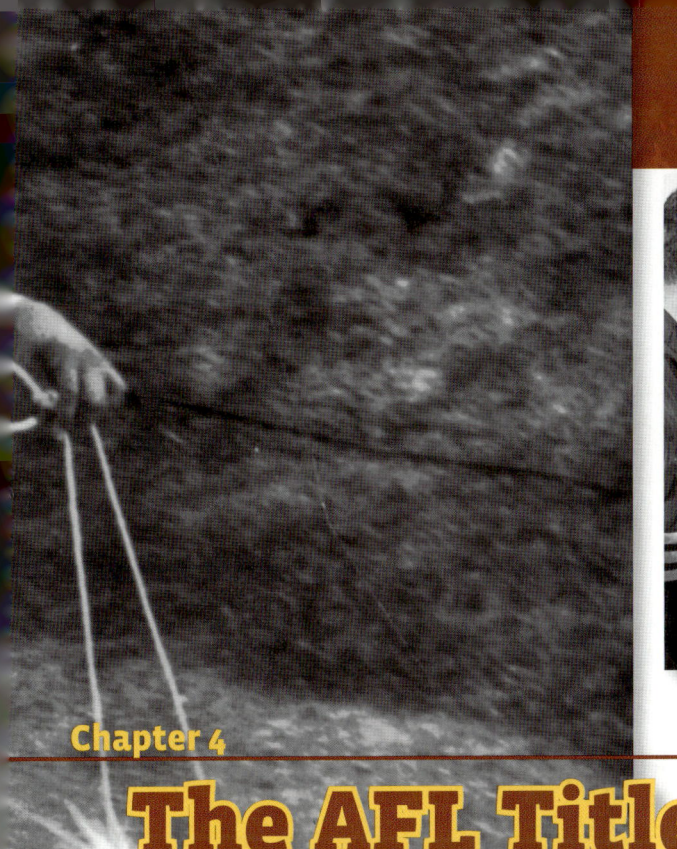

Chapter 4
The AFL Title and Super Bowl I

To get to the Super Bowl, the Chiefs needed to go through Buffalo's War Memorial Stadium on New Year's Day. The conditions were frigid, but the Chiefs were undaunted.

Dawson hit Taylor on a 29-yard scoring strike in the second quarter to put the Chiefs ahead for good at 14-7. The Chiefs intercepted Buffalo quarterback Jack Kemp twice and also forced two fumbles and rolled to an easy 31-7 victory.

That set up a date with the vaunted Green Bay Packers in the AFL-NFL title game, soon to be known as the Super Bowl, in Los Angeles. No one knew, not even Lamar Hunt, the impact on American culture the Super Bowl eventually would have.

"I couldn't have dreamed it," Hunt said. "I don't think anyone could have."

>> *Chiefs fans fondly recall Warpaint galloping the length of the field after every Chiefs score. To the right, pre-game to Super Bowl I.*

The Glory Years 1960-1970 | **31**

> Fred "the Hammer" Williamson talked a good game before Super Bowl I but wound up flat on his back.

Facing Lombardi

The first Super Bowl was scheduled for Jan. 15, 1967, and while it has become common for historians to suggest that there wasn't much hype for the matchup between the Packers and the Chiefs, that is somewhat of a myth. Two networks – CBS and NBC – covered the game. Over 300 media credentials were issued for the game (obviously small by today's Super Bowl standards but remember, this was 1967).

It is estimated that over 60 million viewers observed the contest. Over 60,000 fans – tickets were $6, $10 and $12 -- showed up at the cavernous Los Angeles Memorial Coliseum. About 6,000 of those fans were from Kansas City, it was estimated.

What was at stake was pride. Legendary Packers coach Vince Lombardi often told friends after the game that he felt tremendous pressure to beat the Chiefs. Despite the merger, many of the old guard of NFL owners felt the AFL was inferior. And it was up to Lombardi's Packers to prove it.

"They had everything to lose," Steadman said. "Had we beat the NFL team, Lombardi would not have been king. The (NFL) owners were letting him know, 'You got to win this game.'

> *"For us, it was just get out there and play and try to win."*

Lombardi's players felt he was unsettled by the notion of being upset by an AFL team.

"We didn't know a thing in the world about Kansas City," Packers offensive tackle Forrest Gregg said. "We had never seen them play except on TV. Vince came out and talked to us, and he left no question in our minds that they had a great football team.

"He said, 'You look at the size of the people they have, and you look at the reputation they had before they got into pro football, and then you watch them on film, and you are going to be convinced that your going to be playing a good football team.

"He scared us to death. He really did."**

Packers middle linebacker Ray Nitschke said: "It was the only time I ever saw Lombardi that tense and uptight. I think it carried over to us, especially in the first half. We played tense."

The Chiefs, on the other hand, approached the game as if they had nothing to lose.

"Everybody in the world expected the Packers to dominate us," Dawson said. "But we knew we were a good football team. We didn't see any reason why we couldn't compete."

Some Chiefs even seemed ticked off before the game that the Packers had been deemed such heavy favorites.

Fullback Curtis McClinton said: "This idea of making them a two-touchdown favorite is ridiculous. That is way out of line. The way I see it, they shouldn't be more than a three-point favorite. They get one point for the winning habit, one point because I think they are at the height of their maturity, and one point because they have a strong big-game history."

** *The Packers: Seventy-five Seasons of Memories and Mystique in Green Bay.* Taylor Publishing.

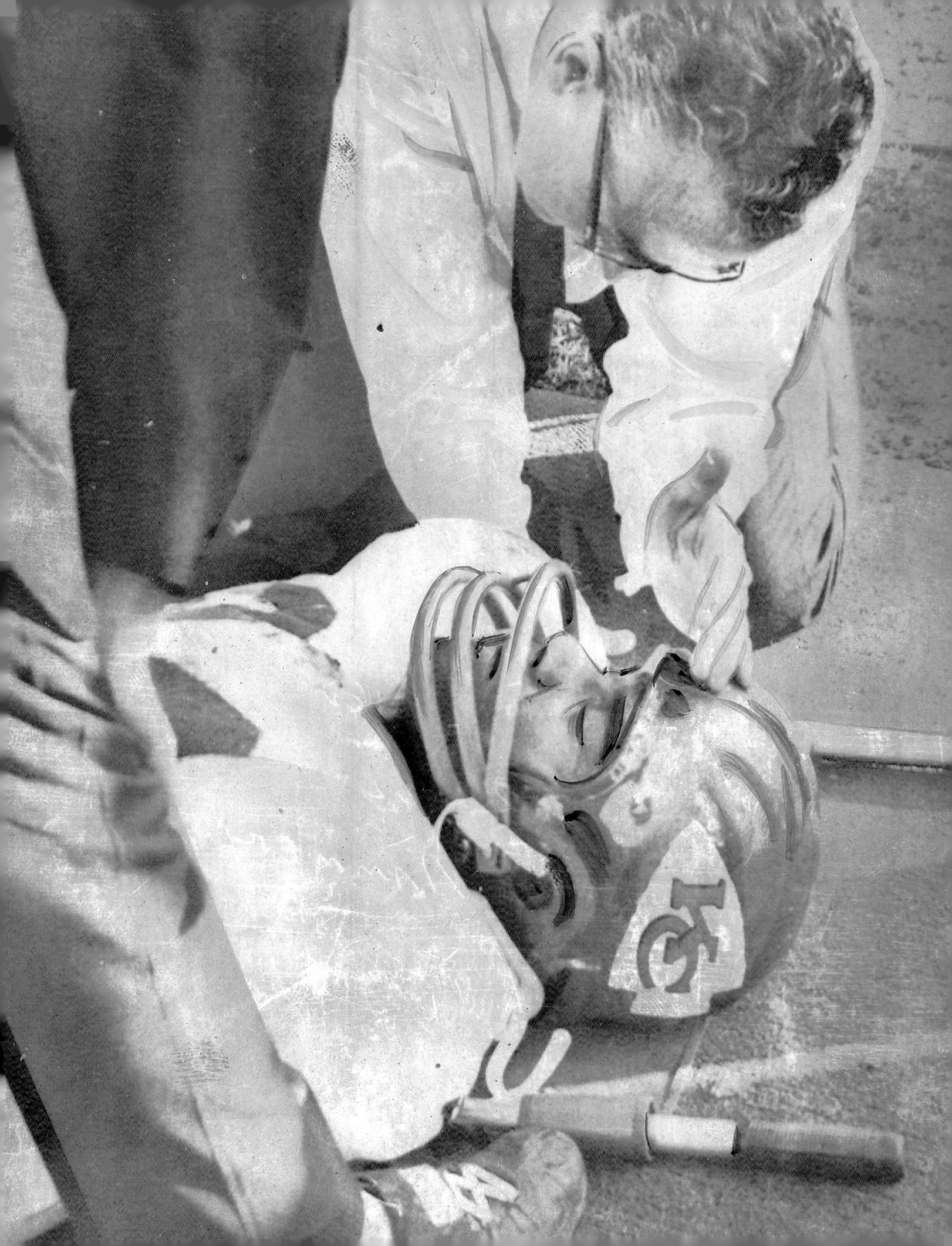

Courtesy of Sports Illustrated

The Game

The Chiefs held their own for the first half.

"We knew they were good up front and had a good rush," Packers quarterback Bart Starr said. "We knew it wasn't going to be easy."

While Starr was the game's Most Valuable Player, the unlikely hero was 34-year-old backup receiver Max McGee. Most fans know the legendary story by now. McGee, not expecting to play, had been out partying all night the previous night. He got back to the hotel just in time to catch the team bus on the morning of the Super Bowl.

McGee had slipped out after curfew on the previous night, ignoring the warning of a $15,000 fine. McGee's reasoning? If the Packers won, which almost everyone predicted, the winning players would receive $15,000 checks. It would be a wash.

"Money didn't mean much to me back then," McGee would say later.

The problem was that the Packers' starting wide receiver, Boyd Dowler, was nursing a sore shoulder. And sure enough, early in the game, Dowler re-injured the shoulder and had to come out. Lombardi barked out, "McGee! Get in there!" A startled and hung over McGee was so frazzled that he grabbed the wrong helmet.

But on the Packers' second possession, McGee made perhaps the greatest catch of his career, reaching back with one hand to pull in a Starr pass and splitting the Chiefs' defense for a 37-yard touchdown. That put the Packers up 7-0.

"The truth is," McGee said, smiling, "it was a lousy pass."

The Chiefs, however, didn't go down quietly, as most observers expected. Quarterback Len Dawson steered his team into Packers territory on the next drive, but kicker Mike Mercer missed wide right on a 40-yard field goal try.

The Chiefs came back again on their next possession highlighted by a 31-yard completion from Dawson to wideout Otis Taylor. Dawson capped off the scoring drive with a 7-yard touchdown pass to running back Curtis McClinton. The game was tied 7-7, and the Packers' bench was nervous.

"We felt like we were right there in it," Dawson would say later. "We felt like we could move the ball. Nobody was intimidated or anything."

The Packers, though, went back on top later in the second quarter when fullback Jim Taylor swept in from 14 yards out to make it 14-7. The Chiefs answered again with a good drive that culminated in a 31-yard field goal by Mercer. The lead was just 14-10 at the half.

> *"I thought by halftime we were going to win the game," Steadman said. "Things came apart in the second half."*

Dawson and the Chiefs were on the move again early in the third quarter, picking up a first down on their initial drive of the half. But then the game turned suddenly on the Chiefs. The Packers had made some defensive

» *Packers running back Elijah Pitts works through the Chiefs defense.*

>> Packers fullback Jim Taylor found a few open holes.

» *The Packers picked up their pressure on Len Dawson in the second half.*

Courtesy of Sports Illustrated

adjustments at the half, and one of them was to call for more blitzing. It was a Packers' blitz that forced Dawson out of the pocket and then to throw a wobbly pass near midfield that was picked off by Packers safety Willie Wood.

Wood returned the pick all the way to the Chiefs' 5-yard line. Running back Elijah Pitts took it from there, and the Packers went up 21-10. The Packers never really looked back.

"It was definitely the turning point," Dawson said. "That changed all the momentum. From that point on, the Packers really turned it up."

Dawson took full responsibility for the bad pass.

"I see quarterbacks make that mistake all the time, trying to make a play rather than take a loss," Dawson said. "Just don't turn it over. They were not known as a blitzing team, but they guessed right on that particular play.

"I didn't have protection on that side. I should have taken off or thrown it away. My arm got hit; the thing fluttered out there. I was backing up, trying to throw it. Not the proper technique. A bad mistake on my part."

Said Stram: "That interception was the key play of the game. It changed the personality of the game. Before that play, and touchdown, we were doing the things we wanted to do. You don't like to think that one play can make that much difference, but it seemed to. From that point on, we had to play catchup. We had to pass more and do things we normally don't do best."

What had been a close game turned into a 35-10 rout. Statistically it wasn't. The Packers only had four more first downs and only 119 more yards of total offense. But few people outside of Kansas City gave the Chiefs or the AFL much credit. McGee, by the way, finished with seven catches for 138 yards and two touchdowns.

Lombardi, who felt pressured by NFL owners to not only beat the Chiefs but also beat them badly, seemed somewhat relieved after the game. Reporters, though, peppered him with questions to compare the Chiefs with other NFL teams. Lombardi, perhaps growing annoyed with the questions, finally said, "The Chiefs are a good team, but they don't compare with the top teams of the NFL. Dallas is a better team. That's what you wanted me to say, isn't it? Now I've said it."

Lombardi said later that he wasn't pleased with that admission. "I came off as an ungracious winner," he said.

The Chiefs came home to Kansas City obviously licking their wounds. But they were still somewhat defiant about the so-called superiority of the NFL and the champion Green Bay Packers.

"They don't hit any harder than anyone else," Chiefs linebacker Sherrill Headrick said. "The thing is, they never block the wrong man – they're always in our way. And their backs always hit the hole. On their sweeps I was getting blocked by a different guy each time – the tight end, the pulling guard, the back. I don't know where they all came from."

› *Lamar Hunt and Hank Stram left the locker room subdued after the Packers won Super Bowl I.*

Revenge

The thumping by the Packers stuck with the Chiefs. Their egos bruised and their pride stinging, the Chiefs got another shot at an NFL team the following preseason. On Aug. 23, 1967, the Chiefs played their first-ever exhibition game against an NFL team – the Chicago Bears – at Municipal Stadium.

"The Bears never had a clue," Dawson said. "They came in here expecting a scrimmage, because we had lost in the Super Bowl and were considered the stupid stepchild. Like Rodney Dangerfield, we got no respect. Well, we had to listen to that crap for seven months, and we were ready. It may have been an exhibition for the Bears, but it was our Super Bowl. It was a chance for us to get some respect." **

The Chiefs blasted the Bears, 66-24, putting up almost 500 yards of offense against the mighty Bears defense led by Dick Butkus. Revenge, for the Chiefs, was sweet.

"Butkus was like a traffic cop," Stram would say later. "All he needed was a whistle and a motorcycle. I remember he said he was afraid we were going to kill that horse (Warpaint, which ran the length of the field after every score)."

**Warpaths*, Taylor Publishing Company

The Final Years of the AFL

The Chiefs didn't have a bad season in 1967 – they were 9-5 and won their last three games. But they were no match for the 13-1 Oakland Raiders, who won the AFL crown but also got thumped by the Packers, 33-14, in Super Bowl II.

Interest in the Chiefs in Kansas City by then was booming. The capacity at Municipal Stadium was increased to nearly 47,000 seats, and Chiefs fans began pouring in to see Len Dawson and the dominating defense.

In 1968, the Chiefs took the city by storm, cruising to a 4-1 preseason record and a 12-2 regular-season mark. Overflowing crowds of 50,000-plus jammed into Municipal that year. The Chiefs' defense, now with Willie Lanier anchored as the middle linebacker, held opponents to 10 points or fewer nine times that season. The Chiefs' offense was balanced, putting up nearly 2,500 yard passing and 2,227 yards rushing.

"We were a complete team," Dawson said. "We could beat you in a lot of ways."

And that included the kicking game. Soccer-style kicker Jan Stenerud, in his second season with the team, scored 129 points. He nailed 30 field goals and was an AFL All-Star.

"No one had seen anything like Jan," announcer Bill Grigsby said. "There were other soccer-style kickers – Jan wasn't the first. But there was no one that good."

As good as the Chiefs were, the Raiders, again, were just as good, if not better. The Raiders also were 12-2. And one of the Chiefs' two losses that season came at the hands of the Raiders, 38-21.

On December 22, 1968, the Chiefs and Raiders met in a divisional playoff game in Oakland to determine which team would play in the AFL title game. It was no contest.

Raiders quarterback Daryle Lamonica threw for 345 yards and five touchdowns against the Chiefs' defense. The Raiders raced to a 21-0 first-quarter lead and blew out the Chiefs, 41-6. Dawson threw four interceptions.

"They just overwhelmed us," Dawson said. "That one stung because they had become our rival and we barely competed that day."

But there was good news to come for the Chiefs and the AFL and especially Lamar Hunt. The Raiders lost to the New York Jets in the AFL title game, and every football fan knows what happened after that.

The Jets, after quarterback Joe Namath guaranteed that his team would win the Super Bowl, did just that and shocked the sporting world with a 16-7 win over the Baltimore Colts. The AFL finally had its measure of respect.

"It meant a lot to every one of us in the AFL," Hunt would say. "Every one of us who took a chance on the new league."

The Jets' stunning upset was just a foreshadowing of more to come for the AFL, Hunt and the Chiefs.

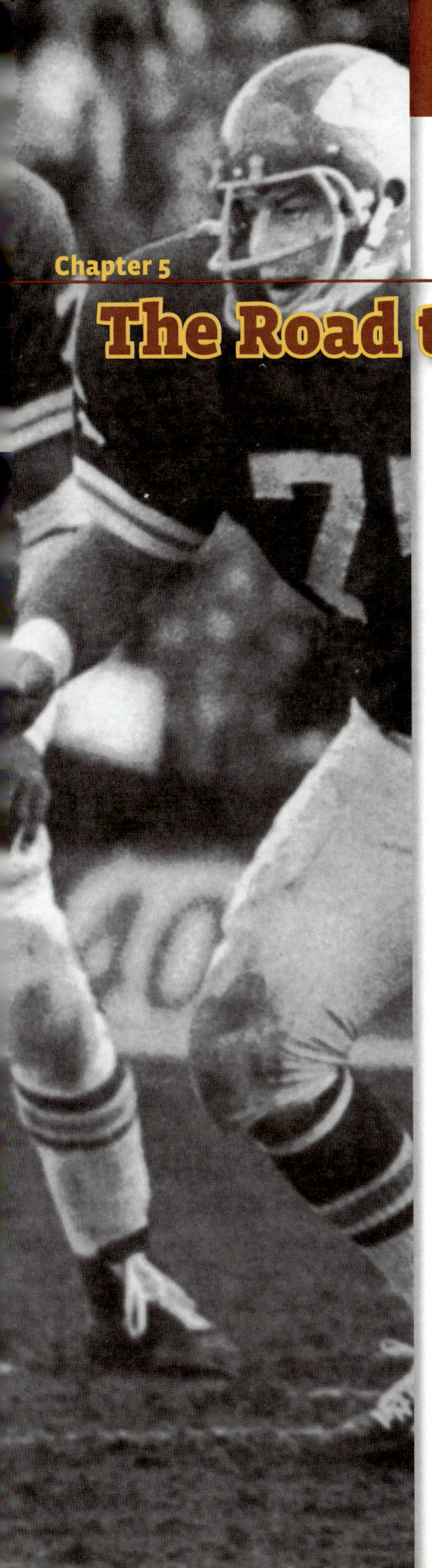

Chapter 5

The Road to Super Bowl IV

The Chiefs again were a powerful group in 1969. They won all six preseason games and nine of their first 10 regular-season games. But the Chiefs had to show some resiliency in 1969. Len Dawson went down with a knee injury early in the season. His backup, Jacky Lee, suffered a broken ankle in late September.

That meant the Chiefs were down to second-year pro Mike Livingston from Southern Methodist. No matter. Livingston guided the Chiefs to six straight wins. Livingston didn't post great numbers – 1,123 yards, four touchdowns and six interceptions – but longtime Chiefs fans will never forget the service he provided the team during this special season.

"I was nervous, obviously, but I just tried to play the game and have fun," Livingston said. "I knew we had a great team around me."

Dawson returned for the final give games, and the Chiefs finished 11-3. Oakland won the Western Division that year at 12-1-1. But the league had approved adding playoff teams, and the Chiefs got into the post-season as the second-place finisher.

The Chiefs' first playoff came against the defending Super Bowl champs, the Jets, at windy and blustery Shea Stadium. The Chiefs hung on for a gritty 13-6 win, thanks to one of the best defensive performances in franchise history. The Chiefs held Namath to 14-of-40 passing and picked him off three times.

But it was an incredible goal-line stand that likely saved the game for the Chiefs. The Jets, down 6-3, had a first-and-goal at the 1 in the fourth quarter. The Chiefs, led by Willie Lanier and safety Johnny Robinson, stuffed the Jets on three straight tries, forcing the Jets to settle for a game-tying field goal instead of the go-ahead touchdown.

Dawson came right back and hit Taylor for a 61-yard gain and then fired a 19-yard touchdown to Gloster Richardson to seal the victory.

"I may have seen better defensive stands," Dawson said, "but none in a game of such importance. That was incredible."

>> *The Chiefs' defense came up with huge plays in 1969.*

The Glory Years 1960-1970 | 43

Courtesy of Hank Young Photography

» *Howard Cosell checked out the Chiefs on the road.*

The win set up a rematch with the Raiders in the AFL title game (the final AFL title game ever). Once more, the Chiefs' defense rose to the occasion – actually, it had to, thanks to a stumbling and fumbling offense. The Chiefs, trying to hang on to a 14-7 lead in the fourth quarter, fumbled three times deep in their own territory. But each time, the Chiefs defense smothered the Raiders.

Finally, Chiefs cornerback Emmitt Thomas picked off a pass and returned it 62 yards to the Oakland 18, setting up a Jan Stenerud field goal to put the game away. Actually, the Chiefs fumbled yet again after that, but the Raiders could not capitalize, and the Chiefs escaped with a 17-7 win.

"We kept fumbling the ball," Dawson said. "Finally, Johnny Robinson came over to me and told me if we fumbled again, don't bother coming back on the field – they'd handle it from there."

The hard-fought win put the Chiefs back in the Super Bowl, in New Orleans, against the NFL champion Minnesota Vikings. To a man, the Chiefs felt confident they could whip the Vikings, mainly because they had beaten them in preseason games the two previous seasons.

"I really felt our Super Bowl game was beating the Raiders," coach Hank Stram said. "If we could beat the Raiders, we could beat anyone. Against the Vikings, I thought we had the advantage because we did so many things offensively and defensively that it would be hard for them to prepare for us in just one week."**

"I felt that if we played Minnesota 10 times, we'd beat them 10 times," Chiefs offensive tackle Dave Hill said. "We knew their offense didn't have a prayer against our defense. Offensively, we felt we could so some things because although they had a quick defense that pursued well, they were not that big."

**Warpaths*, Taylor Publishing

44 | A Sea of Red

Ed Lothamer (82), Ed Budde (71) and Fred Arbanas (84).

» *The Chiefs' secondary, led by Emmitt Thomas (18), was always hungry for turnovers.*

Winning It All

The Chiefs may have been confident, but they were jolted five days before Super Bowl IV when Len Dawson's name, along with other players' names, surfaced in Detroit in a gambling probe by the Justice Department. The story was reported nationally by NBC on the Huntley-Brinkley newscast.

Donald "Dice" Dawson, no relation to Len, was being investigated for his role in nationwide sports gambling. When Dice Dawson was arrested, he happened to have Len Dawson's phone number with him. Len Dawson said he knew Dice Dawson but so did a lot of NFL players. And Len Dawson said he had talked to Dice only once in recent years – not about gambling but about his knee injury and the death of his father.

Naturally, the story created an uproar in Kansas City and at the Super Bowl. Chiefs fans and players thought it was totally irresponsible for Len Dawson's name to be leaked to the media. So did Len.

"You could see what was happening," Len said in later years. "Some politician in Detroit was trying to make a name for himself. But all the report really said was that I might be subpoenaed. So what? They subpoena anyone who might be able to help on a case."

Stram called a meeting before the game to settle his troops.

"I'll never forget that meeting," guard Ed Budde said. "Lenny got up and just looked at everybody and said 'Hey, guys, I wouldn't jeopardize this game for anything.' He didn't have to say anything more. That was the end of it as far as I was concerned."

The story trying to link Dawson to gambling eventually fizzled. And if the rumors distracted anyone, it wasn't the Chiefs, who played like they took out their anger out on the innocent bystanders – the Vikings.

After stuffing the Vikings on the game's opening drive, the Chiefs moved quickly into Vikings territory, and Jan Stenerud booted a then-Super Bowl record 48-yard field goal. Stenerud nailed two more shorter field goals and the Chiefs went up 9-0, appearing in total control.

"I'll never forget seeing the faces of the Vikings, because we were on the

same side of the field, when we sent Jan in for the first field goal of 48 yards," Stram said in later years. "They laughed. They're thinking 'Gee, the coach is goofy.' Jan kicks the ball and they're stunned. They couldn't believe he kicked it that far."

After a Vikings turnover, the Chiefs moved to the Minnesota 5, setting up the play call made famous by NFL Films. Stram instructed his troop to run a "65 toss power trap." The trap blocking confused the Minnesota front four, and running back Mike Garrett strolled in through a huge hole for a touchdown. The Chiefs were up 16-0 at the end of the first half.

"Our game plan was incredible," Dawson said. "I don't think the Vikings knew what hit them."

The Vikings were never a serious threat. After the Vikings pulled to within 16-7 on a Dave Osborn 4-yard touchdown run, the Chiefs went right back to work and moved to the Minnesota 46.

That set up another play captured brilliantly by NFL Films. Dawson stepped back and fired a quick-hitch throw to big-play receiver Otis Taylor. Taylor caught the pass, made the first defender miss and then began to high-step it down the sideline. Taylor pushed away a final defender and waltzed into the end zone. The touchdown put the game away, and the Chiefs went on to a 23-7 win.

The Chiefs were Super Bowl champs. And they did it by being tougher than the Vikings.

» *Few national observers gave the Chiefs a chance in Super Bowl IV, but it was clear from the early going that the Chiefs were the better team.*

Stram talked in later years of safety Johnny Robinson, whose rib and cartilage damage was so severe that he required pain-killing shots before the Super Bowl just to play.

"How he played like he did, I'll never know," Stram said. "But, he did. He made an interception. He recovered a fumble. That was so very special. But then again, all champions are special people. They do unusual things that maybe some people don't, or won't. Those are the types of people that make you win a Super Bowl. We had a lot of people like that.

"(James) Marsalis. Here he is, a rookie, and he starts every single game for us at left corner and does just a magnificent job. Freddie (Arbanas) led in a certain way. Lenny (Dawson) led in a certain way. Willie Lanier, Buck Buchanan in another way. E.J. Holub, he was the holler guy, the agitator.

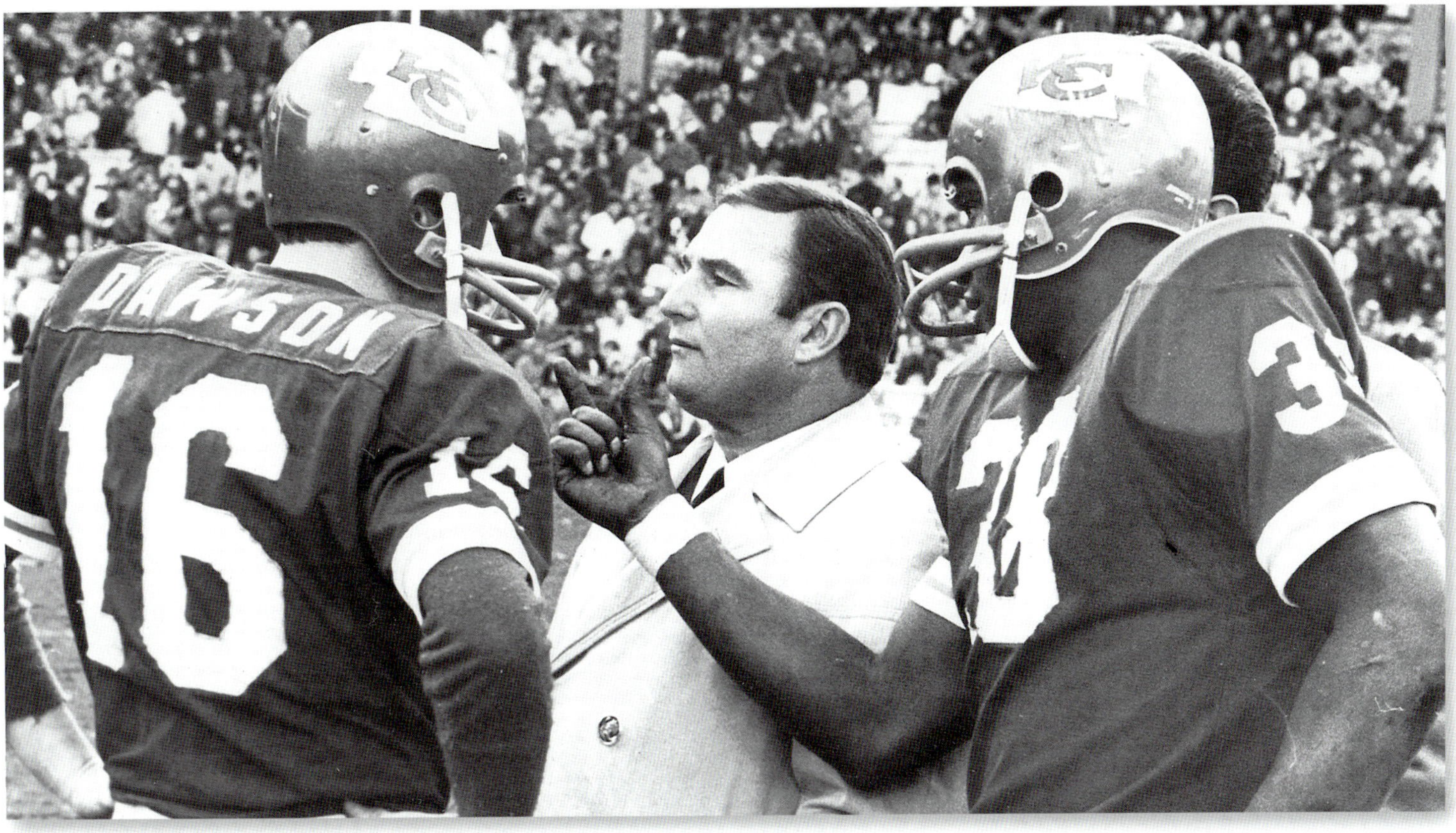
DAWSON
16

» Stram and Dawson each figured they had the perfect game plan to beat the Vikings.

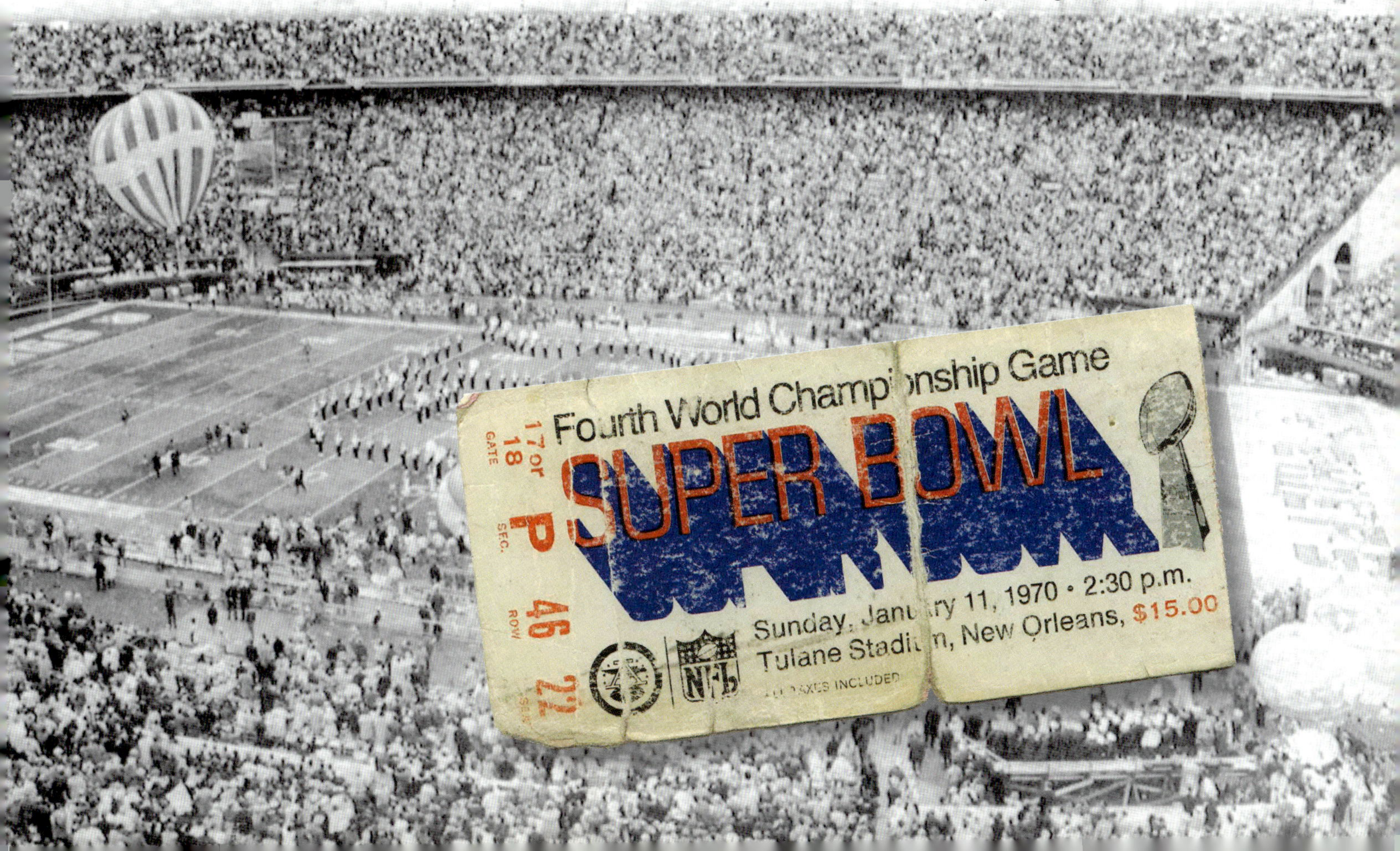
Fourth World Champi onship Game
SUPER BOWL
GATE 17 or 18
SEC. P
ROW 46
Sunday, Janu ry 11, 1970 • 2:30 p.m.
Tulane Stadiu n, New Orleans, $15.00
NFL

» Jan Stenerud (3) started off the scoring with a long field goal, while the Chiefs dominated both sides of the line of scrimmage.

"We just had so many special players and special people."

Dawson, who completed an efficient 12 of 17 passes for 142 yards and one touchdown, was named the Most Valuable Player. It was fitting, for all that Dawson endured before the game. Dawson also took a six-minute congratulatory phone call from then-President Richard Nixon.

Meanwhile, back in Kansas City, Chiefs fans were delirious. Over 100,000 fans welcomed the team back from Louisiana and lined up along the route from Kansas City International Airport to the rally site – Liberty Memorial park. At Liberty Memorial, it was estimated that over 10,000 fans were on hand.

Naturally, Dawson spoke to the crowd and declared, "This is the greatest football and sports town in the world!" The fans screamed with delight.

"There was nothing like it," announcer Bill Grigsby said. "This town was on a high for weeks. Everywhere you went it was like that. It was just a great time, a very special time."

The Glory Years 1960-1970

It was certainly a special time for the man behind it all – Chiefs owner and AFL founder Lamar Hunt.

Hunt was never one to lose the historical perspective of modern events, and he captured it again this time. The Chiefs had won the final game of Hunt's brainchild – the American Football League. The next year, pro football would be realigned with one league, the NFL, made up of an American Football Conference and a National Football Conference.

"It was wonderful to get the satisfaction of winning the final game between the AFL and the NFL," Hunt said. "It was also very satisfying to beat the Vikings, because the Vikings ownership had been one of the six founding clubs of the AFL and had backed out of it after we had our draft that first year. It took us about two months to find a replacement, which turned out to be Oakland.

"From a game standpoint, that certainly was the highlight of my career, but I will never forget the crowd reception and parade when we came back the next day. That was extremely memorable. The enthusiasm of the crowd was amazing."

The Chiefs didn't know it at the time, but it was the end of a special era. The Chiefs' glory years would soon fade. Chiefs fans, however, have never forgotten that time. And they have never forgotten the people responsible for that special time.

Almost two decades later, long after he was done coaching, Hank Stram remembers coming back to Kansas City and walking down a sidewalk on the Plaza.

At one intersection, a man rolled down his car window and shouted, "Hey, coach! Good to see you!"

The same thing happened about two minutes later as another fan smiled and waved at him. Then it happened once more. Stram couldn't believe it.

"I was flabbergasted that so many people stopped," he said. "It was amazing that they would remember."

> **But Stram then thought for a minute and said, "You know ... it was a special time."**

52 | A Sea of Red

The Glory Years 1959-1970

>> *Chiefs fans welcomed the team home and declared the team World Champs.*

The Glory Years 1960-1970 | 55

Chapter 6

The Game that Changed a Franchise

Following the Super Bowl victory, the Chiefs struggled through a tough 1970 season. They lost their final two regular-season games and finished 7-5-2, in second place, one game behind the Oakland Raiders. Len Dawson threw more interceptions (14) than touchdowns (13), and the Chiefs managed two disappointing ties at home to Oakland (17-17) and St. Louis (6-6).

"We were the champions the year before, and every stadium we went into people were sky high for us," safety Jim Kearney said. "I guess everybody was still on that high from the victory parade and having that ring on your finger. That's why it's so tough to repeat."

But 1971 was a different story. The Chiefs soared through the preseason, going 4-1-1, and won five of their first six regular-season games. They

» *Otis Taylor was a part of what might have been the best Chiefs team ever in 1971.*

finished strong, too, winning five of their last six and ending up 10-3-1, easily on top of the AFC West.

Dawson threw for over 2,500 yards and 15 touchdowns. Otis Taylor became the first Chiefs player to top 1,000 yards receiving as he piled up 1,110 yards on 57 catches. In all, 11 Chiefs were named to the Pro Bowl.

Almost to a man, the Chiefs thought their 1971 team was their best ever.

"To me, that 1971 team was better than our Super Bowl team," cornerback Jim Marsalis said. "But that '69 team had one ingredient that the '71 team didn't. In '69, we just refused to be beaten."

The 1971 team did get beaten in perhaps the most crushing loss in Chiefs history.

> **"For 10 years, my Christmases weren't Christmas because of that game. I'm being honest with you. I used to get up Christmas morning and be very irritable and not want to have anything to do with anybody. I would just want to go off and go into a shell. All because of that one game. Every Christmas, it came back to haunt me."**
>
> *– former Chief Otis Taylor*

The 1971 Chiefs couldn't put away the Dolphins in their divisional playoff game, as Miami won 27-24 in the second overtime period of the

58 | A Sea of Red

longest NFL game ever played.

"We were a play or two or three away from winning that game and going back to the Super Bowl," Stram told The Star. "We had so many ways to win that game, it was ridiculous."

Dawson said: "We were better than Miami. I know Miami thought we were a better team, too. But they beat us and went on to the Super Bowl. They started upward, and we started downward."

Maybe if the Chiefs had won that day, they would have gone on to beat Baltimore in the AFC championship game the following week. Then they would have played Dallas in the Super Bowl.

That loss sent the Chiefs into a tailspin.

"It was so devastating," Taylor said. "You would cry and cry and cry, and it didn't matter. You would still ask yourself what you could have done to help us win that game.

"For 10 years, my Christmases weren't Christmas because of that game. I'm being honest with you. I used to get up Christmas morning and be very irritable and not want to have anything to do with anybody. I would just want to go off and go into a shell. All because of that one game. Every Christmas, it came back to haunt me."

» Many of the Chiefs, including Buck Buchanan, thought the Chiefs would make it to more Super Bowls.

For Chiefs, It Really Was 'The Longest Day'

On Dec. 25, 1971, the Chiefs played their final game in Municipal Stadium's 48-year history. A crowd of 50,374 watched the Miami Dolphins prevail with a 27-24 playoff victory over the Chiefs in double overtime.

After 82 minutes and 40 seconds, Miami's Garo Yepremian booted a 37-yard field goal to end it.

To this day, most Chiefs fans consider it the most devastating loss in franchise history.

Harry Jones Jr. wrote in The Kansas City Star the following day: "Not since Billy Graham called for silent meditation at an outdoor religious rally have 50,000 persons been so quiet."

Chiefs kicker Jan Stenerud, arguably the greatest kicker in the history of football and a Hall of Famer, suffered the most painful game of his brilliant career.

Stenerud missed a 29-yard field goal in the second quarter on a play that was supposed to have been a fake kick. With 35 seconds left in regulation, Stenerud could have won it for the Chiefs but missed on a 31-yarder.

In the first overtime, Stenerud had another chance. But his 42-yard effort was blocked.

After the game, Stenerud summed up a city's mood, "I have the worst feeling anyone could have. I have no idea what I'm going to do now. I feel like hiding. ...

"It's unbearable. It's totally unbearable."

Chiefs players, though, stood by their kicker.

"There's no blaming of anyone," linebacker Willie Lanier said. "I missed big tackles. Someone missed a big kick. So what?"

Before the game, the big news surrounding the playoff game was the fact it was being played on Christmas Day – playing on such holidays was unheard of at the time.

Some national columnists called for fans to boycott the game. A Chicago columnist advised fans: "Don't go. Don't watch."

But Chiefs fans ignored the advice. Fans lined up two days in advance just to get standing-room tickets.

The game itself was one for the ages.

An interception by Lanier set up a short touchdown pass from Len Dawson to Ed Podolak, and the Chiefs held an early 10-0 lead. Podolak had one of the greatest games ever, gaining 350 all-purpose yards (85 rushing, 110 receiving and 155 on returns).

Podolak, though, fumbled deep in Chiefs territory just before the half, setting up a tying Miami touchdown.

Neither team gave in during a hard-fought second half. The Chiefs drove 75 yards and took a 17-10 lead in the third quarter. The Dolphins answered with a 72-yard touchdown drive.

The Chiefs roared back with a 91-yard drive, highlighted by a 68-yard pass from Dawson to Elmo Wright. Podolak scored from 3 yards out, and the Chiefs led 24-17 with just six minutes left in the game.

The Dolphins came back, and quarterback Bob

Griese marched them 71 yards, capping it off with a 5-yard scoring toss to Marv Fleming. The game was tied 24-24 with 1 minute, 36 seconds left.

Then, it seemed, the Chiefs were finally going to put the Dolphins away. Podolak took the ensuing kickoff and broke free down the north sideline, racing 78 yards before finally being pushed out of bounds at the Miami 22.

But instead of inching closer for a better shot at the game-winning field goal, the Chiefs ran three conservative running plays and chewed up the clock. The running plays actually lost 2 yards, and the clock was stopped with 35 seconds left and the ball at the Miami 24.

Stenerud pushed the 31-yard kick just wide right. No good.

But the Chiefs won the coin toss in overtime and immediately drove to the Miami 35.

From there, once again Stenerud trotted onto the field for a 42-yard try. But Dolphins middle linebacker Nick Buoniconti leaped high and blocked it.

Later in the first overtime, Yepremian was short and wide on a 52-yard try to win it.

Then in the second overtime, a 29-yard run by Miami's Larry Csonka put the Dolphins on the Chiefs' 36. Three plays later, the Dolphins were at the 30 and on the field came Yepremian. He nailed it, and The Longest Game was over.

Chiefs coach Hank Stram said after the game: "To lose this way, it has to be the toughest loss we've ever had. It's just incredible."

Arrowhead Stadium: The Place to Be

Some fans these days may not believe it, but the concept and the design for Arrowhead Stadium and the Truman Sports Complex were far ahead of their time.

In an era when dual-purpose stadiums were the norm, Kansas City broke the mold in 1967 when voters approved a two-stadium design – one for football and one for baseball. Two-stadium designs then became the norm around the country for decades.

"It really is fantastic to realize how farsighted Kansas City was in the planning of dual stadiums at the crossroads of two interstates," Chiefs owner Lamar Hunt once said. "The concept of two stadiums was absolutely 100 percent right. Other stadiums being built then were in the range of 55,000 to 58,000 seats and dual-purpose stadiums.

"We wanted to go another direction."

The end result for Chiefs fans was the distinctive look of Arrowhead Stadium, a 78,000-seat stadium that many years later became one of the most intimidating places for opponents to play – something that is still true today.

But the completion of Truman Sports Complex didn't come easy. Groundbreaking ceremonies were held in 1968, but two construction strikes delayed the opening by two years.

The project came in way over budget, and both Hunt and Royals owner Ewing Kauffman had to step in and contribute millions just to get the stadiums built.

One of the casualties of the budget overruns was the concept of the rolling roof.

The rolling roof had been the catalyst to excite the public into voting for and approving the bonds needed to finance the project.

"The roof had been such a focus of the campaign that the public felt it had been shortchanged," Chiefs executive Jack Steadman said. "In all fairness, the public was right."

The unique look of Arrowhead Stadium, with its scalloped end zones, almost got scrapped, too. That feature was part of the original design to accommodate the rolling roof.

"We could have saved about $250,000 by squaring off the four corners at the top," Hunt said. "One of our last decisions was, do we save those and the architectural uniqueness? I think it was a wise decision to keep those four corners. It wouldn't look the same."

Arrowhead Stadium was finally ready to be opened on Aug. 12, 1972 for a preseason game against the St. Louis Cardinals. A crowd of 78,190 witnessed a 24-14 victory by the Chiefs.

» Warpaint had different riders through the years but the Chiefs had one bandleader in Tony DiPardo, above.

A Team Adrift 1971-1988

Chapter 7
The End of the Hank Stram Era

The Chiefs muddled through so-so seasons in 1972 and 1973, going 8-6 and 7-5-2, but missing the playoffs both seasons. They finally hit bottom under Stram in 1974 when they finished 5-9, only their second losing season under Stram in Kansas City.

Coincidentally, as the Chiefs moved into their new stadium in 1972, their playing fortunes took a dramatic turn for the worse. Chiefs executive Jack Steadman had given control of most player-personnel decisions to Stram, and the Chiefs' talent base declined rapidly.

"Giving the power to Hank Stram seemed at the time to be a good thing to do," Steadman said. "I was so involved at that point in the stadium development and running the marketing operations that I was spread so thin. As it turned out, it was a bad thing to do."

Not everyone agreed that Stram was given too much control or that he remained too loyal to his older players.

> *"There were a lot of people at the time saying Hank Stram was too loyal and stuck with guys too long," Dawson said. "But that wasn't the problem. I assure you they were the best people at their positions. The problem was that there wasn't anybody capable of taking over for a Bobby Bell or a Willie Lanier."*

Stram was fired after the 1974 with seven years still left on his contract. The way he was fired was highly unusual, too, as Mike DeArmond of The Star recounted in a 1990 story.

In San Francisco to scout players in the East-West college all-star game, Stram got a call from Lamar Hunt and actually took the call in the office of a shop teacher at the high school where the all-stars were training. Hunt told Stram he was making a coaching change. The next day, Hunt made it official by flying to San Francisco and meeting with Stram at the Embarcadero Hotel – Hunt handed Stram a four-page memo that Hunt

» *Right: Willie Lanier anchored the middle of the Chiefs' defense that began fading in the 1970s.*

said would explain the situation better than he could orally.

About a decade later in his book *They're Playing My Game,* Stram blamed Steadman for influencing Hunt's decision based on the fact that Steadman and Stram couldn't get along. Stram also openly admitted ridiculing Steadman's football acumen.

Stram always bristled at the suggestion that he stayed too loyal to his older players instead of restocking the organization with younger players.

"Somebody made that remark once," Stram told The Star in 1990. "But we didn't let it get old. ...If that's what people want to think, that we waited too long, that's fine. But that's not what we did.

"We could adhere to what people said and felt and could try to satisfy what people said – who didn't know what they were talking about. We could have dumped all our players and started all over again.

"But after winning like we did, I didn't want to go through the agony of rebuilding a team from scratch and going 2-14 or 2-12 at the time or 3-11 or whatever. I wanted to infuse talent and continue to win."

Dawson agreed.

» Ed Podolak had a knack for getting the most out of each carry.

"The problem was the people that were playing behind the great players were not as good," Dawson said. "Charlie Getty replaced Jim Tyrer, and Charlie Getty wasn't in the same class as Jim Tyrer. Hank didn't have the people to replace a Lynch or a Lanier, a Bobby Bell.

"I got to the age where players coming in were the age of my children. What do you have in common? Not a great deal. But the real thing was the quality of the team.

"I looked in the huddle when I was ready to retire. It was in Baltimore. I saw Rocky Rasley at guard. Gery Palmer was the other guard. Bill Story was a tackle. Charlie Getty was the other tackle. And I said, 'Who are these people?'"

The end of the Stram era capped off a remarkable run for the Chiefs.

"I remember thinking that there would be so many Super Bowls for us," Lanier said. "I remember a comment from Jack Steadman that sort of crystalized it.

"After the Super Bowl win, a few of us went on to play in the AFL All-Star Game in Houston. We didn't go back to Kansas City with the rest of the team for the parade. We left New Orleans for Houston and missed all of the hoopla back in Kansas City.

"I remember coming back from Houston and Jack saying that next time, we'd all come back to Kansas City for the festivities before going on to the Pro Bowl. Obviously, there was the expectation that it would happen again reasonably soon."

Chiefs fans are still waiting.

» *Podolak shows the wear and tear of playing for a team in transition.*

A Team Adrift 1971-1988 | **67**

The Coaching Carousel

Hunt and Steadman at least knew that replacing a legend such as Stram wouldn't be easy. Due diligence was in order. They sifted through 45 candidates (one of which was Marv Levy) and eventually interviewed 14 candidates. They finally chose Paul Wiggin, a former defensive end with the Cleveland Browns.

But Wiggin inherited a team caught between great players coming to the end of their careers and younger players who simply weren't talented. His teams posted 5-9 marks in 1975 and 1976. And in 1977, his team started 1-6. Hunt had seen enough.

"We have decided in the best interest of the Chiefs to make a change," Hunt told the media at the time. "…We've got seven games left in the season, and we're not writing off this season. We're not satisfied unless we're making every effort to win all those games."

Wiggin, who was replaced by assistant coach Tom Bettis, couldn't believe the firing.

"I was shocked," he told The Star." I never thought I was doing a bad job. I knew things weren't going right, but it's been a tough year – we've had a tough schedule. The bottom line is won-lost."

» *Paul Wiggin wasn't successful as a Chiefs coach but was beloved by the players.*

The Game That Made Ed Podolak a Star

If any good came out of the Chiefs' crushing 27-24 double-overtime loss to the Dolphins on Christmas Day of 1971, it was that Chiefs running back Ed Podolak became an instant celebrity.

Podolak amassed 350 all-purpose yards that game and scored two touchdowns.

"There's no question that the game being on Christmas added to the folklore," Podolak told The Kansas City Star. "Everybody I run into can remember where they were because it was Christmas.

"It helped tremendously with my celebrity status."

Podolak had eight catches for 110 yards, 17 carries for 85 yards, three kickoff returns for 154 yards and one punt return for 1 yard. One of his kickoff returns went for 78 yards and nearly a touchdown toward the end of regulation.

"I don't think any one player in a big game, a monumental game like that, had a day like Eddie Podolak had," Chiefs coach Hank Stram said. "He played with passion, like our whole team did. You talk about playing his guts out – that's exactly what he did."

Dolphins middle linebacker Nick Buoniconti remembers tackling Podolak after a screen pass in the second overtime and slamming Podolak to the ground so hard that Podolak's face mask mashed into torn-up turf at Municipal Stadium.

"I thought he'd get up and be all ticked off at me and cussing me," Buoniconti said. "But we were so dead tired. Eddie just looked at me and said, 'Nick, do you think this game will ever get over?'"

> *Frustration showed on the faces of many Chiefs in 1977, including Tom Condon's.*

Worst Team Ever?

The 1977 Chiefs went on to a 2-12 record and by many accounts might have been the worst team in Chiefs history.

The '77 Chiefs were a team in transition. It was the final season for several remnants from the Super Bowl champion Chiefs of the 1969 season. Linebackers Willie Lanier and Jim Lynch, running back Ed Podolak and punter Jerrel Wilson retired after 1977. The drafts from 1970 to 1975 produced only five players still with the team in 1977.

"We looked awful for a reason," said linebacker Jim Lynch. "We didn't have very good football players. It was so frustrating to put in all that energy and all that effort and still get beat. And not only get beat, but get beat horribly."

Wiggin sensed the Chiefs had bottomed out.

"As the years unfolded, it verified what we had there," he said in later years. "There are a lot of ways a well-run football team can get healed up in the modern world. But in those days, it was strictly the draft, and that's all you had."

Wiggin's firing was immensely unpopular among the players. The firing frustrated center Jack Rudnay.

"Paul Wiggin was a great man and a great coach," Rudnay said. "He gave you your assignment and thought you would do it responsibly. As a veteran, I loved that. ... But we had a lot of young people who ... took Paul Wiggin's attitude as a way to slough off. I'm convinced they got him fired. The veterans worked hard and played hard for him, but he had too many young kids who didn't reflect that philosophy."

Bettis, too, was loyal to Wiggin and didn't want to take the job.

"I was in a no-win spot," Bettis said. "I had looked to possibly having an opportunity of being a head coach, but I didn't feel comfortable with the way it happened. When you're in midseason, I wasn't in favor of taking the job.

"But Paul insisted I take it after they fired him. He said, 'If you don't take the job, this team is liable to fall apart completely.' I changed my thinking. I knew I owed something to the organization and to the players who were still there from the winning years."

But Bettis also went 1-6, and after the season the Chiefs went hunting again for a new head coach.

Free safety Gary Barbaro, in his second year, enjoyed a breakout season with eight interceptions in 1977, and starting in 1980 he appeared in three straight Pro Bowls.

> *"You're not proud of the fact you were part of a 2-12 team," Barbaro said. "What makes it even worse is at the end of the season, I was voted by the players the most valuable player, so I was the most valuable player for the worst team in football. What kind of honor is that?"*

» *Jan Stenerud did get some redemption from the famous Christmas Day loss, beating Miami in 1976 with this kick.*

Getting His Due: Once Unheralded, Thomas Takes His Place Among the Game's Best

The Kansas City Star

CANTON, Ohio | He was a raw rookie from an obscure, historically black college that no longer exists. He was undrafted, unheralded and unpretentious.

So when Emmitt Thomas filled out a standard questionnaire for the Kansas City Chiefs, who brought him into camp in 1966 with about 125 other players, he found one way to grab the club's attention.

QUESTION: What single experience stands out as your greatest in football?

ANSWER: College: Checking Otis Taylor in man-to-man coverage.

The response came as no surprise to Chiefs owner Lamar Hunt. Hunt and scout Wayne Wooley, on a trip to watch Taylor, discovered Thomas' talents as a quarterback/wide receiver and part-time cornerback at Bishop College in Texas in a 1964 game against Taylor's Prairie View A&M team.

They figured if Thomas could limit Taylor, who became the Chiefs' fourth-round draft pick in 1965 and the most-gifted receiver in franchise history, to a paltry three receptions, he could handle the other elite receivers in the AFL.

Thomas did just that. And more.

Blessed with blazing speed and extraordinary hands, Thomas manned the corner for 13 years in Kansas City. He intercepted a club-record 58 passes, returning five for touchdowns, and helped the franchise to two Super Bowls, including a victory in Super Bowl IV.

And in 2008, Thomas was enshrined in the Pro Football Hall of Fame, joining five teammates from the club's Super Bowl years -- quarterback Len Dawson, defensive tackle Buck Buchanan, linebackers Bobby Bell and Willie Lanier and kicker Jan Stenerud -- as well as owner Lamar Hunt and coach Hank Stram.

Thomas ranks ninth on the NFL's all-time interception list and led the NFL with 12 interceptions in 1974 -- two shy of the league record set by Dick "Night Train" Lane in 1952. Thomas also led the AFL with nine interceptions in 1969, the season the Chiefs beat Minnesota in Super Bowl IV.

Thomas made some of his biggest plays on the grandest stages. In the 1969 playoffs, he intercepted a Joe Namath pass in the Chiefs' 13-6 win over the Jets. He intercepted two passes, returning them 69 yards in the 1969 AFL championship game against Oakland, and he iced the Super Bowl win over Minnesota with an interception.

"There was something about me or something about that situation, where I always figured I could make plays, and I was going to make plays," said Thomas, a five-time Pro Bowler. "We had a tall defensive line and three linebackers who could drop back and had pretty good pass coverage skills. I played with Lanier and Jim Lynch on the right side, and we would talk consistently about what was coming and what was going to happen.

"The old AFL was trying to put a product out there to get a TV contract, so they threw the ball a lot, and I had a lot of opportunities."

When Thomas reported to the Chiefs in 1966, he was a raw, lanky wide receiver, and the Chiefs were loaded at the position. They had Taylor, Chris Burford, Gloster Richardson and Frank Pitts.

Once defensive coordinator Tom Bettis saw Thomas run, he asked Stram to move him to cornerback.

"I saw a guy who ran a 4.3 40, and we were looking for speed at the corners," Bettis said. "He had great range, good hands, excellent speed and great anticipation. He was like the seventh or eighth wide receiver, and we were wasting his talent."

The Chiefs had taken four cornerbacks in the 1966 draft, but Thomas quickly made his mark on special teams and as a backup to Fred Williamson.

"I thought I had a good opportunity after a week watching all the other guys," Thomas said. "I was bigger and faster than them. Tom Bettis took an interest in me right off the bat. He saw something in me. He really drilled and worked me hard, stayed on me and molded me."

Still, Thomas was such a long shot, he was issued uniform No. 63 – not exactly a good sign for an aspiring cornerback. After veteran running back Ron Burton was cut, Thomas was given Burton's No. 18.

"When they finally gave me that number," Thomas said, "I thought maybe I had a shot."

Thomas wore No. 18 for the next 13 seasons.

Chapter 8
Marv Levy and the Wing-T

Hunt didn't waste much time going after Marv Levy, whom he'd considered before hiring Paul Wiggin before the 1975 season. Levy had been the coach of the Montreal Alouettes of the Canadian Football League for five seasons and had won two Grey Cup titles.

Hunt made the hire just two days after the season ended in 1977.

But Levy had nearly an impossible task. Essentially, Levy was taking over a team that had less talent than an expansion team.

"The talent base was so bad," Steadman said at the time, "I wouldn't have been surprised if Marv took one look and quit. It made a man want to run away."

Instead, Levy improved the club's performance each year, going 4-12, 7-9, 8-8 and 9-7 in 1981, when the Chiefs narrowly missed the playoffs.

Levy decided his first task was to play more of a ball-control offense. He knew his team was depleted defensively, and he knew he wasn't overloaded with offensive talent.

So Levy employed the three-back, wing-T offense.

"We tried to keep the ball away from the opponents," Levy explained. "That was our best chance to succeed."

Five different running backs put forth 100-yard rushing games. Tony Reed gained 1,053 yards, and Ted McKnight added 627 yards. Overall, the team finished second in the league in rushing. The Chiefs were

74 | A Sea of Red

A Team Adrift 1971-1988 | 75

» Tom Condon was a fixture at guard for the Chiefs before becoming an NFL superagent.

still offensively challenged, particularly at quarterback. Mike Livingston was benched after three games and replaced by rookie Steve Fuller. Livingston eventually was traded to the Vikings.

Levy also was desperate to build a defense. He used the 1978 draft to select defensive ends Art Still and Sylvester Hicks and linebacker Gary Spani.

All of Levy's efforts finally began to pay off in 1980, when the team climbed to an 8-8 mark thanks to wins in two of their last three games. It was backup quarterback Bill Kenney who sparked the wins, subbing for the injured Steve Fuller. Kenney even had a 300-yard passing game in the final contest of the season, creating a feeling in the off-season that the Chiefs might have finally found a quarterback.

In 1981, Kenney emerged as the team's starter, and the Chiefs unleashed another secret weapon – rookie running back Joe Delaney, who quickly became a fan favorite. Delaney was dazzling, running for 1,121 yards and three touchdowns, including an 82-yarder for a score. He also caught 22 passes for 246 yards, including a 61-yarder.

"He was as exciting as they get when he got the ball," guard Tom Condon told The Star. "And the thing people might not remember about him is how tough he was. That guy played with broken ribs and sprained knees, and he was all beat up. But he was tough, like a linemen. He didn't want to come out of a game."

The Chiefs had started the 1981 season 6-2 but slipped down the stretch and narrowly missed the playoffs. But it was clear the team was improving each year under Levy.

But Levy's dream of returning the Chiefs to glory vanished in the strike-shortened season of 1982, when the Chiefs stumbled to a 3-6 mark. Kansas City fans seemed disenchanted with the strike, perhaps more than other cities' fans. In fact, only 11,902 fans showed up for the team's final game on Jan. 2, 1983, to watch the Chiefs pound the Jets, 37-13.

Surprisingly, Steadman and Hunt again gave a coach his walking papers.

Levy said in later years that he had truly given it his all in Kansas City. Levy even had once suggested to Hunt in a 1979 year-end evaluation that to "fully capture fan city spirit, we need a good fight song."

Levy wrote the ditty, "Give a Cheer for Kansas City," which was an imitation of Washington's "Hail to the Redskins."

"I didn't push it," Levy said. "You need to have someone to promote it. I thought it was a good song."

So did Hunt. But it failed to catch on.

And then, after the desultory 1982 season, Levy, with a year left on his contract, was fired in a move Hunt would later regret.

"Marv brought us from nowhere to the point where we were very respectable," Hunt said. "Then, here came the players strike, and our players were out in left field. Marv was extremely supportive of the organization because he was part of management, and we lost the team."

>> *Ted McKnight (22) was an integral part of Marv Levy's Wing-T.*

Hunt and Steadman did not want Levy entering 1983 as a lame-duck coach but could not justify extending his contract after a 3-6 record. Saying the club had reached a plateau under Levy, they fired him.

"You look back on the mistakes you make," Hunt told Randy Covitz of The Star, "and letting Marv go was a mistake."

Levy, who had implemented the conservative, three-back, wing-T offense during his first season with the Chiefs, later flourished in Buffalo with a wide-open, no-huddle, hurry-up offense.

"When we came to Kansas City, there was no intention on my part to stay with that wing-T forever," he said. "We had just an abominable defense, we wanted to keep them off the field. So we controlled the ball.

"The no-huddle was the right approach for that Buffalo Bills team. They had the perfect quarterback for it, and we saw it evolve."

Mike Livingston

Joe Delaney

Chiefs' Fans Never Forgot Joe Delaney

There are certain players who touch the heart and soul of fans. Running back Joe Delaney was one of those players.

Delaney, out of Northwestern Louisiana, was a second-round draft pick by the Chiefs in 1981. He helped energize a Chiefs team that had gone seven straight seasons without a winning record.

But in 1981, Delaney stepped into the starting lineup in the sixth game after Ted McKnight suffered a knee injury. Though only 5 feet 10 and 184 pounds, Delaney proved to be a tough runner inside that complemented his sprinter's speed.

In just 10 starts, Delaney amassed 1,121 yards rushing, at the time a Chiefs record. He had five 100-yard games, including a 193-yard effort against Houston.

Oilers defensive end Elvin Bethea said after that game: "I've played against the best – O.J. Simpson, Gale Sayers, Walter Payton – and (Delaney) ranks right up there with them."

Delaney carried the Chiefs to a 9-7 record.

"He far exceeded anything we expected in terms of ability, in terms of work ethic, in terms of how he comported himself, his team play and the respect he gained from his teammates," said then-coach Marv Levy.

Delaney was the third-leading rusher in the AFC in 1981, made the Pro Bowl as a rookie and was the team's MVP.

Delaney came back in 1982 and led the team in rushing with 380 yards during the strike-shortened season.

Delaney likely would have been a centerpiece for incoming coach John Mackovic's potent offense in 1983.

"He probably had the best outlook for the future as anybody," said Chiefs safety Deron Cherry. "When you come in the league as a rookie and take it by storm, and accomplish the things he did, that says the guy is special.

"We'll never really know what Joe Delaney could have accomplished in a uniform. We just had glimpses."

On June 29, 1983, Delaney was sitting under a tree at Chenault Park in Monroe, La., when he heard the screams of three boys in a nearby pond. Delaney was not a swimmer. But he dived in anyway, fully clothed, and tried to rescue the youths.

Delaney, 24, and two of the boys drowned, while another boy made it back to safety.

The Chiefs wore a patch on their uniforms in 1983 to honor Delaney, and owner Lamar Hunt declared that no other Chiefs would wear No. 37 again.

In 2004, Delaney was inducted into the Chiefs Hall of Fame.

» *Even during the down years, the Chiefs boasted a talented secondary led by Lloyd Burruss (34) and Gary Green (24).*

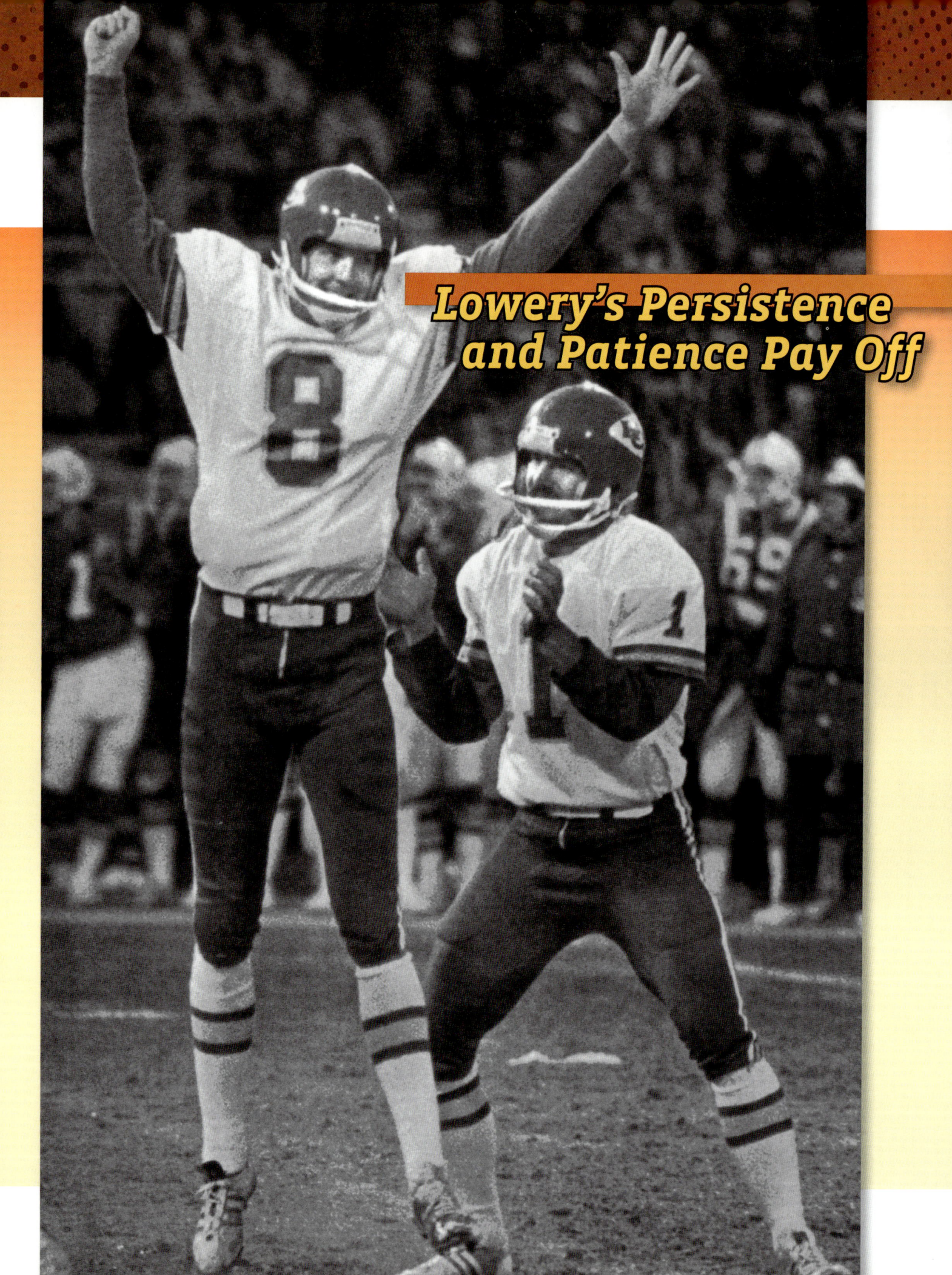

Lowery's Persistence and Patience Pay Off

The 39th member of the Chiefs Hall of Fame stands out among his peers for one reason -- his resolve.

"None of the others were cut 11 different times by eight different teams," Denny Thum, interim Chiefs president, said. "While that may not sound like a badge of honor, it certainly speaks to the perseverance of one Nick Lowery."

Lowery, the Chiefs' kicker from 1980 through 1993, is still their all-time leading scorer.

Overcoming his inability to establish himself as an NFL kicker wasn't Lowery's biggest challenge on joining the Chiefs. He also had the daunting task of trying to unseat Jan Stenerud, who would later become the first and only kicker in the Pro Football Hall of Fame.

But Lowery did so and went on to kick in three Pro Bowl games. Only Will Shields played in more games for the Chiefs than Lowery's 212.

"Keeping Nick was clearly a controversial move, but there's no question (then-head coach) Marv Levy made the right decision," Thum said.

Lowery initially declined the Chiefs' offer to attend training camp in 1980. He later changed his mind because he believed his 12th NFL tryout would turn out different.

"I was so much stronger physically and emotionally, so I felt ready," said Lowery, who now lives in Arizona.

"Here I was going against Jan Stenerud, but I had come so far. I remember telling Clark Hunt, who was a 16-, 17-year-old ball boy and charting me every day, that I felt I had to outdo him every day, but I felt ready. It was all about timing."

As the years passed without Lowery being selected for the Chiefs Hall of Fame, he began to wonder whether the honor would ever come. But in 2009, he got the call he had waited for from Len Dawson.

"The wait was even worth it," Lowery said. "It's such an honor to have Len Dawson call me up and ... welcome me to the Hall of Fame. An honor like this is fantastic whenever it comes. You think about the people that came before you like Buck Buchanan and Derrick Thomas and Mack Lee Hill, who aren't with us any more, and Lamar Hunt. You appreciate it because life is short.

"What I try to do is think of all the names up (on the Arrowhead Stadium facade), the people that deserve to be up there, the sacrifices they made, the pain many of them live in today that I don't have to deal with at nearly the same level. It's a real blessing.

"It's the greatest honor you could have. Obviously, the NFL Hall of Fame is a wonderful honor, but to be recognized by your own team is sort of like (being recognized by the) family you went to war with and the people you care about the most."

-- Adam Teicher

>> *Lloyd Burruss, left, and Gary Spani (59), below, always had a knack for finding the ball.*

84 | A Sea of Red

» Even during the down years, the Chiefs had weapons on offense, such as wide receiver Henry Marshall (89), and on defense, such as Burruss, Kevin Ross (31) and Deron Cherry (20).

A Team Adrift 1971-1988 | **85**

The Mack Attack

Hunt and Steadman this time reached for what they thought was a flashier coach – handsome Dallas Cowboys quarterback coach John Mackovic. It was Mackovic who proclaimed that the NFL had become a passing league and that to be competitive, the Chiefs needed to throw the ball far more efficiently.

But even before Mackovic's first game, the Chiefs were struck with tragedy when Joe Delaney drowned while trying to save three youngsters in Monroe, La. The franchise and the entire Kansas City community were stunned by the sad news.

Mackovic pressed on, even with the loss of his top offensive weapon. The Chiefs traded Steve Fuller to the Rams, and Mackovic announced that Bill Kenney's heir apparent would be Todd Blackledge, whom Mackovic had selected with the ninth overall pick in the 1983 draft.

Selecting Blackledge turned out to be one of the most second-guessed decisions in team history – the Chiefs had passed on Jim Kelly and Dan Marino in that draft.

Mackovic delivered on an early promise – the Chiefs passed and passed often. Kenney attempted 603 passes in 1983 and threw for 4,348 yards and 24 touchdowns. Carlos Carson had 1,351 receiving yards. Deron Cherry and Lloyd Burruss emerged as one of the top safety duos in all of football. But the overall lack of defense crushed the team's chances, and Mackovic finished 6-10 in his first season.

The Chiefs' dominating secondary was solidified in 1984 when corners Albert Lewis and Kevin Ross joined Cherry and Burruss. The team improved to 8-8 in 1984 but a seven-game losing streak in the middle of the 1985 season doomed them to a 6-10 mark.

"We couldn't make any strides climbing the mountain," nose tackle Bill Maas said. "We tried so many different things – different approaches, different off-season programs, everything – figuring that this would make a difference. But nothing did. We had a lot of individual talent, but when we came to being a team, we never succeeded."

Then came the improbable 1986 season.

For a team that hadn't made the playoffs since 1971, the 1986 season provided a rare thrill.

"It was one of the highlights of my career," Lewis told Kent Pulliam of The Star. Lewis blocked four punts in 1986 and helped the team surge to a 10-6 record and a playoff spot.

Stephone Paige (83) set the Chiefs' record for receiving yards, 309, in one game against San Diego in 1985.

Three straight wins to close out the regular season pushed the Chiefs into the post-season. In those three weeks, the Chiefs beat Denver 37-10 behind Blackledge, who was filling in for Kenney, beat the Raiders in Los Angeles 20-17 and beat the Steelers 24-19 in Pittsburgh by scoring all their points from special teams.

"That team that went to the playoffs was a team that saw an opportunity and rose to the occasion," Maas said. "But it was a team that really wasn't prepared to go the playoffs. I don't think we were ready."

The '86 Chiefs were cruising at 7-3 toward a division title when they dropped three straight and suddenly needed to win out to make the playoffs. It was a team built on special teams and defense, not on Mackovic's passing offense. Mackovic had hired Frank Gansz as his special teams coach for 1986, and special teams responded with a season for the ages. Equally as important was the defense directed by Walt Corey. The defense forced 49 turnovers.

» *Dino Hackett (56), above, wasn't afraid to throw his body around. Art Still (67) was a fixture at defensive end for a decade.*

"But we never had an offensive identity on that team," offensive tackle Irv Eatman said. "One week we would be a passing team, and the next week we were a running team."

The playoffs came down to a final game in Pittsburgh. But with Kenney again nursing injuries, as was much the case that year, the offense was inconsistent. Enter Gansz' special teams.

Burruss scored the winning touchdown of the game, returning a blocked field goal by Maas for 78 yards. Boyce Green also returned a kickoff 97 yards for a touchdown, and Cherry recovered a blocked punt by Lewis in the end

zone for another touchdown. Despite being outgained 515 to 171, the Chiefs beat the Steelers 24-19.

The Chiefs, after a painfully long absence, were finally back in the playoffs.

The celebration was short-lived. The Chiefs ventured to New York to play the Jets, and with Blackledge at quarterback, it was no contest. The Chiefs took an early lead but the Jets rolled to a 35-15 win in what turned out to be Mackovic's last game.

» *The Chiefs toasted making the playoffs in 1986, and fans supported them even after the playoff loss.*

» The Chiefs took an early lead in the 1986 playoffs but wound up being no match for the Jets.

» Chiefs fans and Chiefs players had little to celebrate after a 35-15 loss.

A Team Adrift 1971-1988

» Chiefs fans became increasingly angry in the late 1980s, even taking their ire out on Bo Jackson, then a Raider.

» Frank Gansz was regarded as perhaps the best special-teams coach in football. But he didn't fare as well as the head coach.

The Player Revolt

Within just a few days after the rout by the Jets, there was more trouble back in Kansas City. Gansz stunned the team and fans by announcing his resignation in order to seek "better opportunities." There were also rumors that Corey was going to do the same.

Soon after, eight members of the Chiefs reportedly met with Hunt to express their concern about losing Gansz and Corey.

Hunt responded by firing Mackovic and subsequently hiring Gansz as the new head coach of the Chiefs. Hunt later denied that the meeting was an anit-Mackovic session and suggested this his primary concern was to simply keep the coaching staff intact.

Ironically, however, Corey left anyway, and joined Levy who had taken the job as head coach of the Buffalo Bills after he was fired by the Chiefs.

Gansz' stint as the Chiefs head coach was nothing short of disastrous. He went 4-11 in 1987 (one game was lost due to a players' strike) and 4-11-1 in 1988.

Big changes, though, were on the Chiefs' horizon. On Dec. 8. Steadman resigned as the team's president and was later named chairman of the board. General manager Jim Schaaf was fired on Dec. 8. And Gansz was fired on Jan. 5, 1989.

The moves all made room for a new regime and an exciting new era in Chiefs football.

Part III: A Team for Kansas City 1989-2009

Chapter 9

Peterson-Schottenheimer Era Restores Hope

The Chiefs had virtually become an afterthought on the Kansas City sports landscape when Carl Peterson took over as general manager in 1988.

The Royals were just a few years removed from winning a World Series title, and sports talk in Kansas City focused on the Royals first. The Chiefs were a distant second.

Season-ticket sales in 77,622-seat Arrowhead Stadium had plummeted to 26,000 upon Peterson's arrival.

But that was soon to change.

Within just a few years, the Chiefs became the talk of Kansas City. A Chiefs game became the event to attend.

Even in the Chiefs' glory years, Kansas City had never seen anything like it. Nearly 80,000 fans started jamming into Arrowhead Stadium each

> Owner Lamar Hunt introduces his new general manager, Carl Peterson.

Sunday in the 1990s. The parking lots were a sea of red and barbecue smoke before games. Everyone started talking Chiefs football.

How did Peterson do it? He cleaned house. Quickly.

Peterson, who helped construct a Super Bowl team in Philadelphia and built a two-time United States Football League champion from scratch, totally overhauled the franchise, from changing head coaches to installing a computerized ticket system.

Peterson hired a new coach and also replaced nearly every high-level person in the front offices.

"Of nine directors," Peterson once said, "I replaced seven of them.

"This might get me in trouble. But one of the things I perceived when I came here, and also looking from the outside in, I felt one of the possible reasons for this franchise not doing well was people ran over everyone here.

"I told Lamar Hunt, `If there was a perception previously that this club could be a pushover, I want that to cease.' Now whether you call that arrogance or confidence or an attitude, I believe that. And that begins not only with your competition on the field but with agents, players, coaches, administration - whoever it might be."

Peterson also switched the Stadium Club caterer, the airline, the car dealer, the phone system, the ticket system, the training campsite, the radio station, the groundskeeper - even the mascot.

Peterson's first order of business when he took the job, of course, was to decide on what to do with then-coach Frank Gansz.

"I told Frank and the staff I would take a couple of weeks and go through every game of the season and even some from the season before and try to be objective and make a decision on their performance," Peterson said. "It's not always the coach's fault. It would have been an easy rationalization or excuse that every time it's a poor year on the field, we'll fire the coach and get a new head coach, and things will get better.

"Besides making a judgment on whether this guy will be a successful coach in the NFL is that we're in the entertainment business, and sometimes you need to bring some new faces in."

Peterson decided Gansz wasn't the right fit and fired him.

The next step was to hire Marty

» Peterson, in turn, later introduced his new head coach, Marty Schottenheimer. Together, they turned around the franchise.

» Peterson's first significant player move as GM was picking linebacker Derrick Thomas in the draft.

Schottenheimer, who had become disillusioned in Cleveland and resigned as coach of the Browns.

"Marty brought with him a couple of the things that made the decision easier for me: the success he experienced as a head coach in four years at Cleveland, and the advantage of being able to bring a majority of his staff with him," Peterson said. "You don't have to re-coach your coaches. You can hit the ground running.

"The other aspect was how we would get along. I felt very comfortable. He knew me and

my reputation, and he knew I was going to give him anything necessary to win."

Peterson then turned his attention to the draft and selected Derrick Thomas with the fourth pick of the 1989 draft.

"I believe you build defense first; you win with defense," Peterson said. "We could have taken (linebacker) Broderick Thomas, too. And we often wonder if Detroit hadn't taken Barry Sanders and Derrick had gone third in the draft, what would we have done there? It would have been easy to take Barry Sanders.

"Derrick pretty much had to be an impact player. I don't like to put that much pressure on any rookie, but we needed help on defense immediately, and that was the obvious reason for taking him."

Peterson, Schottenheimer and Thomas: The foundation was now set for what would turn out to be an incredible run for the Chiefs in Kansas City.

» *Schottenheimer was a standout special-teams player with Buffalo, above left. Schottenheimer with his wife, Pat, far left. Schottenheimer's staff included Bill Cowher, pictured here with Kevin Ross.*

» Schottenheimer loved veteran quarterbacks, such as Steve DeBerg and Ron Jaworski, above, but wanted to build his team around defense, especially Derrick Thomas.

» The Chiefs had a powerful running game in the early 1990s with Christian Okoye (35) and Barry Word (23).

A Team for Kansas City 1989-2009 | **101**

Virtually Unstoppable: Derrick Thomas' 7-Sack Game

If there's such a thing as a pass rusher being in a zone, Derrick Thomas was in one.

In a 17-16 loss to the Seattle Seahawks at Arrowhead Stadium, the Chiefs' linebacker had the best pass-rushing performance since the NFL began recording individual sacks in 1982. He sacked quarterback Dave Krieg seven times, breaking the single-game record of six set by the 49ers' Fred Dean in 1983.

Thomas was oh, so close, to an eighth sack, and that would have changed the game's outcome. Krieg squirmed out of Thomas' reach on the last play of the game and threw a 25-yard touchdown pass to Paul Skansi, which tied the score before Norm Johnson's kick.

That pass took all the joy out of Thomas' record-breaking day.

"I would've felt a lot better had we won the game," Thomas said.

"Maybe 10 or 20 years down the road, I'll look at it as a major accomplishment. But right now it lingers in my mind as a loss."

Thomas' third-quarter sack of Krieg, his third sack of the game, forced a fumble that was recovered in the end zone by Dan Saleaumua. That gave the Chiefs a 16-10 lead, which they held until the final play.

and Schottenheimer were looking to pump more offense into the attack. That's when Peterson acquired veteran Dave Krieg.

But while Krieg had his moments in 1992 (he threw for 3,115 yards but threw 12 interceptions and had a pedestrian 79.9 passer rating), it became clear to Peterson and Schottenheimer that Krieg might not be the answer, either.

The Chiefs mustered a 10-6 mark in 1992 and made the playoffs yet again. But the offense was completely stymied at San Diego in the wild-card playoff game, and the Chargers rolled to an easy 17-0 win.

» *Al Saunders, above, a receivers coach under Schottenheimer, eventually became Dick Vermeil's offensive coordinator. Under Peterson, the Chiefs made the training-camp move to River Falls, Wisconsin.*

A Team for Kansas City 1989-2009

» John Alt (76) was one of the best tackles in the game, while Dale Carter (34) certainly had the talent to be the best corner. To the left, the Chiefs are welcomed by the people of River Falls, Wisconsin.

» Derrick Thomas enjoyed being an active part of the Kansas City community and charity scene.

» Thomas, below, and Neil Smith look dejectedly at the scoreboard during a playoff loss at San Diego.

» *Dan Saleaumua was a fan favorite on the defensive line.*

Chapter 10
Greatness Arrives

The Chiefs stunned the football world in April 1993 when they completed a deal with the 49ers to acquire Joe Montana. Anyone in the NFL who wasn't quite aware of the Chiefs' resurgence had to pay attention now.

And Peterson wasn't through. In June of that year he landed another legend – running back Marcus Allen.

"This is the one guy Marty wanted from the first day of free-agency," Peterson said at the time. "This is a player and person we have had to play against for too long."

Allen quickly had to address concerns that at 33, he wasn't a weapon anymore in the backfield.

"All I want from Marty is the opportunity to play," Allen said "I'll show you what I can do. All I want is a chance to compete, and that's all I was promised."

» Everyone wanted to get a peek at Kansas City's new celebrity.

A Team for Kansas City 1989-2009 | 111

It's a Deal – Finally! Chiefs Get Montana!

By Kent Pulliam
The Kansas City Star
April 21, 1993

It's official.

Joe Montana will be wearing a Chiefs uniform next season. The on-again, off-again negotiations ended about 6:30 Tuesday night when the Chiefs and the 49ers agreed upon a trade that brings to Kansas City the highest-ranked passer in NFL history. Montana is one of only two winning quarterbacks in four Super Bowls.

The deal involves another player and two draft choices. Terms of the trade will be announced at a news conference today at the 49ers' headquarters in Santa Clara, Calif.

The Chiefs will give up their No. 1 choice in Sunday's NFL draft, according to reports in San Francisco. In return, the Chiefs will receive a player, reportedly safety David Whitmore, and San Francisco's No. 3 draft choice in 1994. The Chiefs would not comment on the trade details.

After the news conference in San Francisco, Montana will leave for Kansas City. He could be on the field as early as Thursday morning, when the Chiefs' off-season program continues.

"I think we are all pleased that it has finally been agreed upon," said Carl Peterson, the Chiefs' president and general manager. But he cautioned fans against expecting too much. "I am not going to put any pressure on Joe Montana that he has to work miracles. Our hope is that he can help us take another step in regards to the improvement of the Kansas City Chiefs. If we didn't feel he could do that, we wouldn't have made these efforts."

The Chiefs have been pursuing Montana since April 6. Twice during the last four days the 49ers publicly said they had broken off negotiations with the Chiefs. The 49ers also said repeatedly that they favored the deal offered by the Phoenix Cardinals.

Montana, who will be 37 at the start of next season, holds the NFL record for highest completion percentage in league history, connecting on 63.7 percent of his passes over a 13-year career. He has passed for 35,124 yards and thrown 244 touchdown passes.

» *The acquisition of Montana by Peterson stunned the football world.*

He holds the NFL record for the highest single-season passer rating with a 112.4 mark in 1989, when he completed 70.2 percent of his passes and threw 26 touchdowns. He was intercepted just eight times that year. On two occasions he has completed 22 consecutive passes.

He has been the NFL Most Valuable Player twice (1989 and '90) and was MVP of the Super Bowl three times. Only Montana and Pittsburgh's Terry Bradshaw have been the winning quarterback in four Super Bowls. Montana also has been selected to play in the Pro Bowl seven times.

Injuries have hampered him in recent years. He missed most of the last two seasons because of elbow problems. His replacement, Steve Young, led the 49ers to the best record in the NFC last year and was selected the league's Most Valuable Player.

Montana played only the last half of the 49ers final regular-season game last year, and he threw two touchdown passes.

After the season, Montana was told he would not be given a chance to regain his starting job, but he was not given permission to talk with other teams until the 49ers signed backup quarterback Steve Bono on April 6.

Montana came to terms with the Chiefs last Friday night. He didn't change his mind even after a weekend meeting at the home of 49ers owner Eddie DeBartolo Jr. DeBartolo, a close friend of Montana's, told him the 49ers would reinstate him as the No. 1 quarterback if Montana remained with the team. Instead, Montana announced Monday that he wanted to keep his commitment with the Chiefs.

"I thought there was a possibility, and a strong one, that they would make one last attempt to keep Joe a 49er," Peterson said. "I didn't believe at any time in this whole scenario that Joe would not have to sit down with the owner of the 49ers and make his peace. That was really going to be the test of his decision to come to KC.

"I really respect Joe and his wife, Jennifer, for staying with their commitment and their decision. They obviously felt very good about it, and they stayed with it even when the 49ers came back to see if Joe would remain."

Peterson said Montana told him that he was anxious to begin working with the Chiefs in their off-season program.

» *Montana hurls the winning touchdown pass in the final seconds of the Chiefs' dramatic Monday Night Football win over Denver.*

"He wants to get involved with our receivers and our offense and (offensive coordinator) Paul Hackett," Peterson said. "This is what he wanted to do. He asked me how long this would take when we came to agreement on a contract, and he was anxious to get going."

The move is similar to others Peterson has made since arriving in Kansas City, bringing in established and successful veterans to help improve his club - beginning with longtime All-Pro center Mike Webster and veteran quarterback Ron Jaworski in 1989.

"The obvious is that this guy is a four-time world champion at the most important position on the offense, quarterback," Peterson said. "With our new offense - one he is extremely familiar with - it's a major plus for both Paul Hackett, our offensive coordinator, and our quarterbacks.

"They (our fans) are going to have expectations, but I would hope they are also realistic that Joe Montana has not participated in the last two years."

The football world indeed took notice.

Before Montana arrived, the Chiefs were headed in the right direction. The team had made the playoffs three straight seasons, and ticket-sales were booming. But Montana, and Allen, made the Chiefs not only national, but international.

Montana and Allen took the Chiefs to a new level. Their star power along with Thomas' star power made the Chiefs a show.

In fact, in Montana's two seasons with the Chiefs, they were on national television six times. Montana's presence completely overtook Kansas City – starting in 1994, the Chiefs led the league in attendance (averaging 76,650 fans) for six straight seasons.

On the field, Montana still had some magic left. His body struggled to maintain the punishment of the NFL, and he was injured often. But in 1993, Montana still threw for over 2,000 yards and 13 touchdowns. He led the Chiefs to an 11-5 record and their first AFC West title under Schottenheimer.

Montana also guided the Chiefs to a dramatic 27-24 overtime win over Pittsburgh in the first round of the playoffs. The next week, few experts gave the Chiefs a chance to win at Houston. But Montana engineered a stunning 28-20 upset. The ride finally ended the

» *Offensive tackle Joe Valerio (73) scored on several tackle-eligible plays.*

following week at Buffalo, when Montana was knocked cold in the second half and the Chiefs were blitzed 30-13.

Still, Chiefs fans without question had Montanamania. And the feeling carried into 1994, especially when Montana faced his former team, the 49ers, at Arrowhead in September. Montana also was facing the man who replaced him in San Francisco, Steve Young.

The game was hyped as if it were a Super Bowl. The attendance nearly reached 80,000 at Arrowhead, and they did not go away disappointed – the Chiefs prevailed 24-17.

Later in the regular season, Montana was matched up against Chiefs nemesis John Elway and the Broncos at Mile High Stadium on Monday night. In one of the most exciting finishes in Chiefs history, Montana hit Willie Davis with a 5-yard touchdown with eight seconds left to lift the Chiefs to a 31-28 win.

But Montana could not lift the Chiefs past the first round of the playoffs that year as they fell at Miami, 27-17. It turned out to be Montana's last game as a pro – he retired shortly thereafter.

Allen hung around and led the Chiefs in rushing the next two seasons. He also scored 11 touchdowns on the ground in 1997 before finally retiring.

» *The Chiefs and Montana stuck it to Warren Moon and the Oilers, but Montana was knocked out by Marv Levy's Buffalo Bills.*

» Two legends, Dan Marino and Joe Montana, meet, below, after Montana's final game.

The Pain

Montana's backup in 1994, Steve Bono, took over the quarterbacking duties in 1995, and the Chiefs hardly missed a beat. In fact, thanks to some spectacular special teams play – Tamarick Vanover returned three kicks for touchdowns – and an opportunistic defense, the Chiefs were magic on their own without Montana.

The Chiefs won 10 of their first 11 games in 1995; three of those wins came in overtime. The team cruised to a 13-3 record, good enough for a first-round bye. They eventually met the Indianapolis Colts at frigid Arrowhead in January of 1996 in what turned out to be one of the most crushing losses in team history. The offense sputtered, and Bono was intercepted three times in a 10-7 loss. But most fans in Kansas City pinned the loss on kicker Lin Elliott, who missed field goals of 35, 39 and 42 yards. The last miss came in the final seconds. To this day, it is a loss that haunts Chiefs fans. It was also Elliott's last game as a Chief.

Though most of the blame for the playoff loss went to Elliott, Kansas City fans turned on Bono the following year when the Chiefs stumbled to a 9-7 mark. Bono was picked off 13 times in 1996 and had a woeful 68.0 passer rating. His remarks about San Francisco's

» Kicker Lin Elliott missed three field goals against the Colts and virtually became public enemy No. 1 in Kansas City.

» *Rich Gannon came in for Steve Bono and put the Chiefs in a position to tie the game.*

restaurants being better than Kansas City's didn't sit well with the locals, and by 1997, Peterson and Schottenheimer ushered in yet another San Francisco product at quarterback – Elvis Grbac.

Grbac did score some points with Chiefs fans with an incredible comeback win over Oakland on Monday Night Football, when he hit Andre Rison in the closing seconds for the winning touchdown. But even as the Chiefs were rolling to another dominating 13-3 season – again sparked by great defense and special teams as Vanover had two more returns for touchdowns – many Chiefs fans began pulling for backup Rich Gannon to be the starter.

Again the Chiefs held home-field advantage in the playoffs and this time faced the Broncos at Arrowhead on Jan. 4, 1998. Grbac couldn't get the Chiefs in the end zone more than once, and Kansas City suffered yet another agonizing loss at home, 14-10.

Super Bowl dreams again went up and smoke, and it became apparent to most observers that the Chiefs' window of opportunity was closing.

By 1998, the foundation that Peterson and Schottenheimer had built began to come undone. The Chiefs bickered in the locker room and on the field, and they set NFL records for penalties (158) and penalty yards (1,304).

» *Before there was Dante Hall, Tamarick Vanover was a sensational return man.*

≫ *Steve Bono took over for Montana but never won the hearts of fans.*

"HE DID IT JUMPING ON AND OFF THE RICH GANNON BANDWAGON."

A Team for Kansas City 1989-2009 | 125

» Elvis Grbac had his moments, but many fans preferred Rich Gannon.

» Andre Rison helped the Chiefs to a 13-3 record in 1997.

» *The devastating playoff loss to the Colts was just the beginning of the heartache. The Chiefs also came up empty in the final moments of their playoff loss to Denver.*

Deluge and Lightning Force Delay of Chiefs' Game

The Kansas City Star
Monday, October 5, 1998

In more than 35 years of pro football in Kansas City, the Chiefs had never seen a storm like the one that slammed into Arrowhead Stadium on Sunday night.

Hard rain swirled and severe lightning flashed from the first moment of the Chiefs' nationally televised game against the Seattle Seahawks. The result was a 54-minute lightning delay, the first of its kind at Arrowhead, and a sloppy game finally won by the Chiefs 17-6.

Play was stopped at 8:14 p.m. -- almost an hour after it began -- with the game tied 3-3. Before the game resumed at 9:08, players adjourned to the locker rooms and fans were cautioned to leave the upper-deck seating for the safety of the lower concourse.

Even Paul Tagliabue, National Football League commissioner, was notified and kept apprised of the situation throughout the storm.

"This was the worst I've ever seen," said Art McNally, NFL assistant supervisor of officials, who called the delay. "We had some lightning go across the sky, and in my judgment, the last that we saw was severe enough and too close to the stadium.

"I felt that it was time to pull everybody out. We cannot take a chance with the safety of the players and the fans in the stands."

The weather service reported 3.6 inches of rain fell downtown between 7:15 and 9 p.m.

Weather had never been the cause of a delay at a Chiefs home game, although a preseason game against the Bears at Chicago in 1992 was suspended in the third quarter because of lightning. The last NFL game to be canceled was New England at Miami on Sept. 6, 1992, with Hurricane Andrew the culprit.

On Sunday, the thunderstorms rolled in around 7:15 p.m., and five minutes later, with ESPN featuring the Chiefs-Seahawks as its Sunday night game, Seattle kicked off. Puddles formed in a matter of minutes.

By the time Chiefs kicker Pete Stoyanovich slipped and fell, tying the game with a 22-yard field goal near the end of the first quarter, the field was a sloppy mess. Paint from the Chiefs' logo at midfield was fading. The "Chiefs" lettering painted in both end zones was washing away, and the "Huskers" and "Cowboys" lettering from Saturday night's Nebraska-Oklahoma State game reappeared.

"The field has had enough," Andre Bruce, Arrowhead head groundskeeper, said during the first quarter. "We knew there was going to be some rain, but we didn't know it was going to be this much. But this is football, and that is what the field is for."

Conditions were much improved after the delay. Fans could finally remove their raincoats and ponchos. And the teams could actually attempt forward passes, something that happened only seven times in 37 offensive plays before the stoppage.

During the delay, some fans gathered in the concourse, while others sat in the rain. Four ran onto the field and tried to dodge security for a thrill. One sprinted from the 50-yard line to 5-yard line before being tackled. All were escorted off the field in handcuffs.

Among the 66,418 fans who attended Sunday's game, more than half waited out the delay. Stewart Littlefield, 33, and Brian Palcher, 27, both of Kansas City, Kan., sat shirtless in the rain hoping the game would resume.

"They shouldn't have called the game. This is what football is all about," said Littlefield, a longtime season-ticket holder. "This is definitely my most memorable Chiefs game."

Chapter 11

The Marty-Carl Breakup

Rumors began circulating about Schottenheimer's future near the 1998 season's end, and shortly after the final game, Schottenheimer announced he was stepping down as coach.

He said his biggest disappointment was not getting Lamar Hunt back to the Super Bowl.

But he didn't have to look far to find his greatest satisfaction.

"See those seats," a choked-up Schottenheimer said, pointing through a window at the Arrowhead Club while announcing his resignation. "All those people. ... You can't buy it. The fans. The greatest fans.

"I always thought the Dog Pound was pretty good when I was in Cleveland. But these people are the standard-bearers, in my view, of the fans that make a difference. That is clearly the greatest thing that I will remember about my time here."

Schottenheimer will always be remembered as the coach that turned an organization around. The Chiefs' record in the 15 years before him was 86-137-1.

"He totally changed the entire momentum of a generation of losing with the Chiefs," said Bill Maas. "He helped our team in a manner of one year to learn how to win, through the work ethic to win and how to expect to win."

>> *Schottenheimer helped revitalize a franchise but by 1998 the magic had faded.*

A Team for Kansas City 1989-2009 | **133**

» Lamar Hunt announces Marty Schottenheimer's departure.

Schottenheimer guided the Chiefs to a 101-58-1 record, three AFC West titles and one AFC championship game among seven playoff appearances in 10 years. And Arrowhead Stadium filled to the brim.

"It was a golden era of Chiefs football," Hunt said.

Only the San Francisco 49ers, at 123-37, fared better than the Chiefs during 1989-98.

Peterson didn't look far for Marty's replacement, selecting defensive coordinator Gunther Cunningham.

"This last year the Chiefs lost their way a little bit," Cunningham said upon taking the job. "I think it's like walking through a forest. We took the wrong path. There is no doubt in my mind where the right path is."

Peterson defended his decision by saying: "I don't see the necessity of complete turnover."

But while Cunnigham's players were extremely loyal to him, he never did find that "right path."

Cunningham's team lost its final two games in 1999 to finish 9-7 and miss the playoffs. The killer was an overtime loss to Oakland, 41-38, in the season finale. The Chiefs weren't any better in Cunningham's second season, finishing 7-9 in 2000, leading to yet another coaching change.

》 *Many believe Schottenheimer lost control of the 1998 team. Here, Derrick Thomas publicly apologizes for the Chiefs' Monday Night Meltdown in 1998 when the Chiefs set an NFL record for penalties.*

» *Carl Peterson introduces Gunther Cunningham, seated with his wife, Rene, as the new coach.*

» *Gunther Cunningham wanted a power running game with Bam Morris.*

Forever a Chief: We Never Got the Chance To Say, 'Thank You'

By Jason Whitlock
The Kansas City Star
February 9, 2000

Thank you, Derrick Thomas. Thank you for touching our hearts. Thank you for touching our children's lives. Thank you for the joy you brought us on NFL Sundays. Most of all, thank you for teaching us how to deal with adversity.

Derrick Thomas, the soul of the Chiefs for 11 years, left us Tuesday morning. Complications from his single-car accident Jan. 23 caused his death.

Sudden death.

We never had the time or the opportunity to thank Derrick properly.

A private plane whisked Thomas home to Miami the day after his SUV flipped on Interstate 435. Miami's Jackson Memorial Hospital specializes in treating spinal-cord injuries and paralysis. Thomas went home to prepare for the fight of his life. He was surrounded by family, blood relatives, lifelong friends, the men and women who turned a hard-knock kid into a man of unlimited compassion and desire to do right.

Back here, we anxiously awaited news of his recovery, looking forward to the opportunity to welcome Derrick back to his adopted home.

We thought we'd have time and the opportunity to tell Derrick just how much we loved him, just how much we cared for him as a man, not as a superstar linebacker.

Never has a last thank-you seemed so important. The suddenness of Thomas' death is a second tragedy more cruel than the first. We had prepared for the long fight that faced Thomas. We had contemplated ways we could help.

There was no way to prepare for this. There was no way to anticipate a late-morning phone call saying that Thomas had passed, and so had our last opportunity to tell Derrick just how special he was.

When the Derrick Thomas book is written, it should be about a man who overcame every obstacle life dealt him except one.

"It's a story about a kid who basically came from nowhere, from the streets, and turned out to be a great man in this society," Thomas' high school wrestling coach, Wilbert Johnson, whispered into the phone Tuesday evening. "I'm proud of everything Derrick accomplished. I'm glad I played a small part in his life."

Thomas was born on the first day of 1967.

His parents were poor, young and unprepared for the responsibility of raising a child. His father, Robert Thomas, later joined the Air Force, became a pilot and in 1972 was shot down and killed in Vietnam.

Obstacle No. 1 -- no father.

Obstacle No. 2 was his mother's youth. Unready

for the responsibility, Thomas' mother, Edith Morgan, left her son in the care of her mother, who lived in Perrine, Fla., a tiny, economically depressed city just outside Miami.

"Perrine is the kind of place you don't want to raise a family," Ransom Hill said a couple of weeks ago. Hill grew up in Perrine. He lived just a block away from Thomas' grandmother. Hill is the principal of MacArthur South Alternative school, where Thomas landed for a few months after graduating from Dade Marine Institute, the day school Florida's juvenile courts banished Thomas to after he ran afoul of the law.

Hill took notice of Thomas' athletic ability. He contacted friends at South Miami High and suggested that Thomas finish his final two years of school at South Miami, where he could play sports. Hill also suggested South Miami because he knew the coaches there would keep Thomas out of trouble.

Thomas wasn't the star of his high school football team. Another linebacker, Keith Carter, received most of the acclaim and attention from recruiters. Poor grades scared many recruiters away from Thomas. Alabama was one of just a handful of Division I programs to offer Thomas a scholarship. And Thomas had to attend summer school to qualify academically.

He became a star at Alabama, where he was a two-time first-team All-American.

Carl Peterson and Marty Schottenheimer used the fourth-overall pick in the 1989 NFL draft to select Thomas. Troy Aikman, Tony Mandarich and Barry Sanders were selected ahead of Thomas.

Of course, we know what happened when Thomas arrived here. His speed pass rush was the foundation of a defense that led the Chiefs to a decade of consistent winning and playoff appearances. He was selected to nine straight Pro Bowls. His community service and Third and Long Foundation, a literacy program for children, earned him the 1993 Edge NFL Man of the Year award.

A rough and controversial 1998 season, which included his infamous "Monday Night Football" meltdown and temporary loss of his starting job, caused Thomas to mature on and off the field. He handled the adversity of the 1998 season the way he handled adversity throughout his life: head-on with a commitment to turn a negative into a positive.

A year ago, he bought a commercial roofing company. He ran the company himself five days a week, even during the season. He said the extra work gave him focus and limited his time for mischief. Known as the NFL's "social chairman," Thomas slowed his nightlife carousing. He had a plan and was well into changing himself from football star to former football player turned businessman.

On Jan. 23, Thomas and two friends, Mike Tellis and John Hagenbusch, hopped in Thomas's SUV. Thomas and Tellis were catching a plane to St. Louis. They were going to watch the second half of the NFC championship game and celebrate with the Rams afterward. Hagenbusch was going to drive Thomas' SUV back to Thomas' Independence home.

Thomas' vehicle hit a patch of ice, skidded and flipped out of control.

Thomas was lucky to have survived the crash. Tellis, Thomas' longtime friend, died at the scene. He and Thomas were thrown from the vehicle. Hagenbusch, the only one wearing a seat belt, walked away from the crash with minor injuries.

Thomas spent two weeks and a day in Miami. According to friends, he had already planned his return to Kansas City. He wanted to rehab here. By mid-March, Thomas wanted to be back in his Independence home. Friends had begun preparing his home for his arrival.

"Boss Man 58" wanted back in his castle. He bossed his friends and loved ones from his hospital bed. "Derrick was Derrick" became the catch phrase when someone who had seen Thomas would describe his mood, his attitude. He hated hospital food, so he had his family bring him food from home.

The toughest part of the accident for Thomas had been the death of Tellis. Thomas was in remarkably good spirits about his own injuries. Friends would break down and cry at the sight of him immobilized or in a wheelchair, and Thomas would cheer them up.

"Come on, now. I'm not going to be like this forever," he would say.

"God has a plan for all of us," Wilbert Johnson said. "It seems like it takes death to make us immortals."

The High-Flying Dick Vermeil Show

The first thing that became obvious when Peterson hired his old friend, Dick Vermeil, to coach the Chiefs was that fans would see some excitement again. There would be offense, and plenty of it.

Vermeil brought in a quarterback he knew well from his days with the Rams, Trent Green, and Green knew the offense that Vermeil and offensive coordinator Al Saunders operated. Although Green threw 24 interceptions in Vermeil's first season in 2001, Green also threw for 3,783 yards. The Chiefs also unleashed a new weapon in the backfield, Priest Holmes, who would emerge as one of the top threats in football. Holmes ran for 1,555 yards in 2001.

The Chiefs finished just 6-10 in 2001, but won three of their last four games. They improved to 8-8 in 2002 as Green threw for 3,690 yards and 26 touchdowns. Holmes added another amazing season, rushing for 1,615 yards and 21 touchdowns. And the Chiefs unveiled yet another weapon – returner Dante Hall.

Hall electrified Chiefs fans by returning two punts for touchdowns and a kickoff for a touchdown.

But as amazing as the Chiefs were offensively – they scored 467 points in 2002 – they were just as abysmal defensively. The Chiefs surrendered 399 points in 2001.

Then came the spectacular 2003 season. The Chiefs burst out of the gate and won their first nine games. There was talk of a perfect season. Holmes ran for 1,420 yards and scored 27 touchdowns on the ground. Green threw for over 4,000 yards. And Dante Hall became perhaps the most thrilling player in football.

Hall returned two more punts for touchdowns

and two more kickoffs for touchdowns. Hall simply terrified opponents, who tried desperately to kick away from him. Hall also scored on a 67-yard pass reception.

The Chiefs rolled to a 13-3 record and gained a first-round bye, setting up a home playoff game with the Indianapolis Colts. Sound familiar? These Colts were far different from the version that broke the Chiefs' hearts in a 10-7 win years earlier. These Colts had Peyton Manning and Marvin Harrison and Reggie Wayne and Edgerrin James.

The Chiefs threw everything they had at the Colts offensively. Holmes rushed for 176 yards and two touchdowns. Green threw efficiently for 212 yards and one touchdown. Hall, again, did his thing – returning a kickoff 92 yards for a touchdown in the second half.

But the Chiefs simply couldn't hang with Manning and company. The Colts rolled up 434 yards against a pitiful Chiefs defense and held on 38-31. Once more, the Chiefs' Super Bowl dreams were dashed.

The Chiefs continued to dominate offensively in 2004 and 2005 under Vermeil. Green threw for over 8,500 yards during those seasons. Larry Johnson took over for Holmes as the starter in 2005. He rushed for 1,750 yards and had 20 rushing touchdowns. Hall returned three more kickoffs for touchdowns during those two seasons.

Future Hall of Fame tight end Tony Gonzalez caught 102 passes for 1,258 yards and seven touchdowns in 2004. He had 78 catches for 905 yards in 2005.

A Team for Kansas City 1989-2009 | 143

But Vermeil and Peterson couldn't fix the woeful defense, and the Chiefs finished 7-9 and 10-6 and missed the playoffs both seasons.

When asked about the huge gap in talent between the Chiefs' offense and defense, Vermeil defended his and Peterson's personnel decisions.

"When you're a head coach, you have to care about both sides of the ball equally," he said. "Sure, I grew up as an offensive coach. But that goes away when you become head coach. … Believe me, I think about defense more than I think about offense because we have so many new guys. I'm probably watching them even more closely."

Said Peterson: "For many years here, we had a coach, Marty Schottenheimer, who always thought defense. Toward the end of his time in Kansas City, Marty said he would concentrate more on offense. But he really couldn't do that. He's a defensive guy.

"Dick is an offensive guy. It's in his blood. Obviously he understands defense. He knows that we have to get much better on defense this year if we want to achieve our goals. But when he thinks, he thinks like an offensive coach."

Again, Peterson seemed forced to find a new coaching philosophy, and he turned to former defensive back Herm Edwards to take over as head coach of the Chiefs for the 2006 season.

Edwards brought a military-tough attitude to coaching, and an old-school philosophy to offense. Edwards had Johnson carry the ball a staggering 416 times in 2006. Johnson ran for 1,789 yards and 17 touchdowns, and the conservative approach paid off as the Chiefs sneaked into the playoffs on the final day of the regular season with a 9-7 record.

But the Chiefs' offense couldn't move the ball at all in the opening round of the playoffs at Indianapolis and fell somewhat sheepishly, 23-8, to Peyton Manning.

Edwards, though, had no intentions of piecing together a so-so team each season, hoping to sneak into the playoffs. Edwards persuaded Peterson to blow up the roster and start from scratch. The Chiefs' officially went "young" under Edwards and filled the depth charts with rookies behind rookies.

Predictably, the team struggled. The Chiefs finished just 4-12 in 2007 and bottomed out at 2-14 in 2008.

Chiefs fans weren't buying into the youth movement, and Clark Hunt, who had taken over the franchise's operations after the death of Lamar Hunt, felt it was time to make a change at the top.

» Eddie Kennison, above, catches the game-winner in overtime to beat the Packers in 2003. Dante Hall, right, was the scariest return man in football.

» *The playoff shootout at Arrowhead between Peyton Manning and Trent Green was a joy to watch. But in the end, the Chiefs couldn't keep up with the potent Colts.*

A Team for Kansas City 1989-2009 | 147

148 | A Sea of Red

Holmes and Dad Both Strive to Touch Lives

By Joe Posnanski
The Kansas City Star 2003

This is an old, old story. A father explains to his son why he has to go to war. Only, in this story, the father is in his 50s — even the son is not quite sure how old. The father has already spent a full life working and raising a family and going to church and high school football games and giving his spare time for 27 years to the Army Reserve.

The father has spent the last couple of years in uneasy retirement, showing up at neighbors' houses to fix things, keeping up with his three grown children, including his son, who just happens to be the best running back in pro football.

"I don't get it, Pops," Priest Holmes remembers saying. "You've done so much already. Why go now?"

"It's something in my heart," Herman Morris explained.

Next month, Herman Morris will go to Iraq with his reserve unit. He volunteered to go awhile ago, long before President Bush called up the Reserves. As a short answer, he calls it a sense of duty. He will be based just outside of Baghdad for a year, and his job will be to find ways to move supplies — from ammunition to water — across a chaotic country.

He knows it's dangerous work; all work in Iraq is dangerous.

He knows there are not many 50-something men volunteering to go to Iraq.

He also knows that it's important.

"It's not something I expect everyone can understand," Herman Morris said. "I really feel like it is something I was called to do."

No, Herman did not expect everyone to understand. But he wanted his family to understand, particularly his son, Priest Holmes.

"I told him that he didn't have to explain," Priest said. "I told him, 'Pops, you're a grown man; you've raised your family; you've worked hard all your life. You do what's in your heart.' And he said, 'No, I need you to understand.'"

"It was important to me that Priest know where I was coming from," Herman said.

Herman is the only father Priest has ever known. He married Priest's mother, Norma, when Priest was 4. Herman taught his son how to play chess. He showed his son the importance of hard work. Those are two of the driving forces in Priest's life.

The two men just formed a deep bond. They are so similar — modest, devoted, quiet and yet forceful.

"He's just a good man," Priest said of his father. "I've learned a lot about being a man from him."

"I see a lot of myself in Priest," Herman said. "He's the one I thought could understand."

People always compare football and war. Football coaches almost universally admire (and compare themselves with) generals like Patton. Players often call themselves soldiers. Little themes of war are everywhere in football. George Carlin pointed out years ago that in football, field generals mix aerial assaults and ground attacks to march into enemy territory, even if it means using bombs, bullets and the shotgun.

"I told Priest that going to Iraq is dangerous and a little bit scary, but we work together and do what we're told, just like in football," Herman said.

And they talked for a while about the satisfaction of being part of a team, looking out for teammates, thinking about the whole group.

"I told him that I could see that feeling in this year's Chiefs," Priest said. "In the past, maybe everybody had individual goals that were not connected to winning. Now, though, everybody's goals are about winning."

But, of course, when it comes down to it, football and war are very different.

"I don't like it when people call football players 'heroes,'" Priest said. "Those people who fight for our country, those are the real heroes. They are the ones who put their lives on the line for our freedom."

So, Priest Holmes asked his father the obvious question: He asked Herman if he was afraid. Herman Morris said he was a little bit scared, sure, but only a little bit.

"Then why go?" Priest asked.

"This is what we've trained for," Herman said. "I'm ready for this."

They talked for a long while about Priest's journey. Herman was there every step. Priest blew out his ACL while at Texas. He was a backup running back in college. He was not taken in the NFL draft. Herman Morris can remember when Priest used boxes as furniture while he tried to make a name for himself in Baltimore.

And yet, all along, Priest Holmes refused to give up on himself.

"What was it that kept you going?" Herman asked him.

Priest said part of it was faith, of course. His mother, Norma, is devoutly religious — she did, after all, name her son Priest. Then there was a part of him that wanted to prove everyone wrong. That's just his nature. The more someone says he cannot do something, the more he wants to do it. He learned that from Herman, too.

"You can't let anyone else," Herman said, "tell you what you can't do."

But Priest told his father there was something else, too. Something harder to describe. There was this unquenchable belief he felt that this is what he was meant to do. It did not matter how many coaches told him he was too small or too slow or too brittle. He just knew that he was supposed to play football.

"It's hard to me to explain that to some people," Priest Holmes said. "But I just believe I was given a gift. And I believe that I can touch people's lives with my gift."

"That," Herman Morris said, "is the exact same reason why I have to go to Iraq."

And with that, Priest Holmes nodded.

"I think he understood," Herman said. "I really think he understood."

» *The Colts and Peyton Manning and Edgerrin James were simply too much for a porous Chiefs defense.*

» *Fans loved Jared Allen, who here grabs hold of Michael Vick.*

» Dante Hall was no doubt one of the most exciting Chiefs players to watch.

A Team for Kansas City 1989-2009 | 155

» Herm Edwards took over for Dick Vermeil, and the Chiefs' offense immediately took on a more conservative approach. Edwards hoped Brodie Croyle would be his quarterback of the future, but Croyle being carted off was a familiar scene.

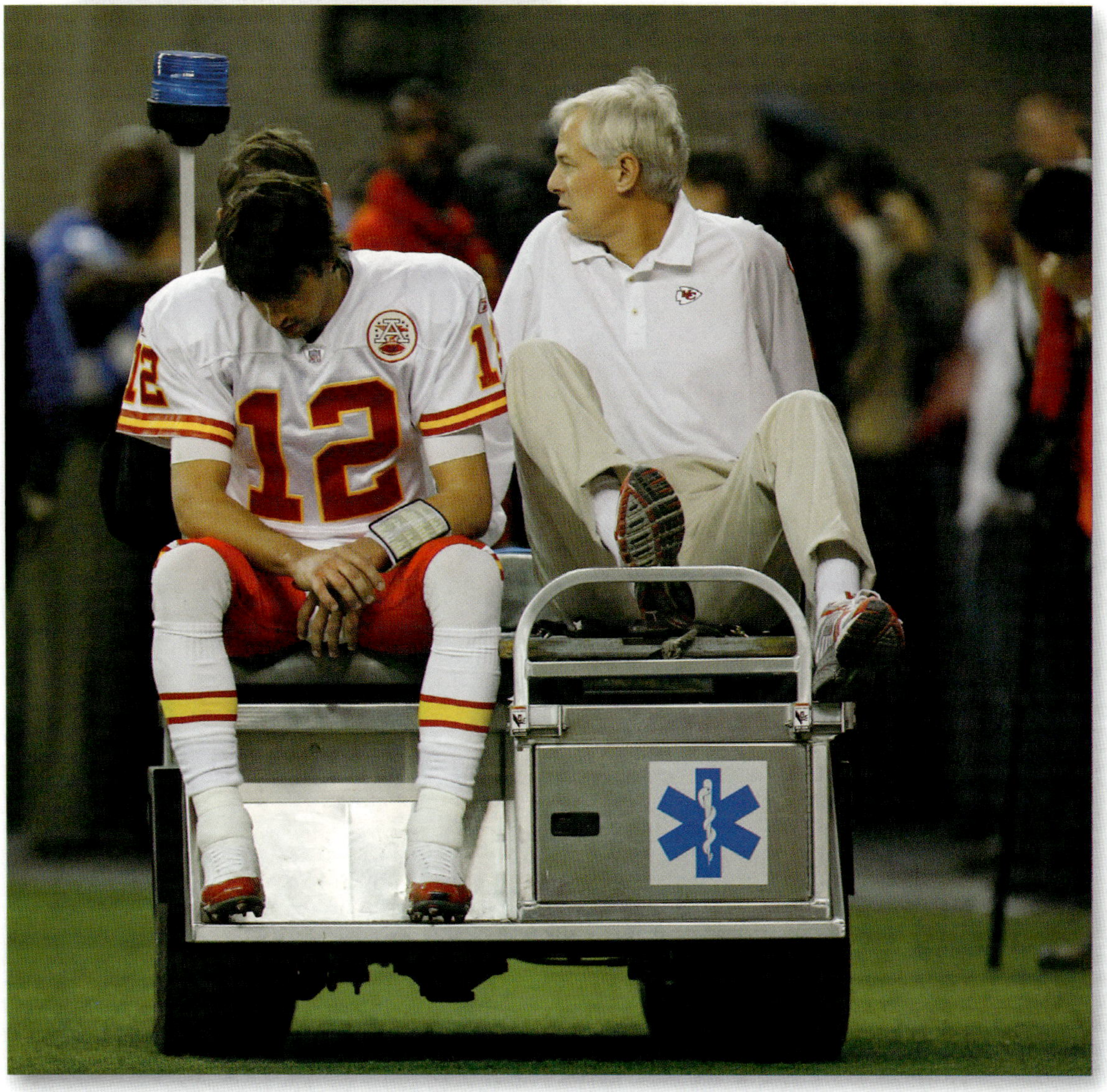

» Two of the NFL's best at the time: LaDainian Tomlinson and Larry Johnson.

> The Chiefs' pitiful offense didn't muster a first down until late in the third quarter against the Colts in 2007 and fell, 23-8.

158 | A Sea of Red

Lamar Hunt, 1932-2006
'He Changed Our Way of Life'

The Kansas City Star
Thursday, December 14, 2006

Lamar Hunt was a sportsman. A visionary. An entrepreneur. A gentleman. And a bit of a rebel.

Hunt, founder of the Kansas City Chiefs and one of America's most innovative and creative sports figures of the past half-century, died about 9:40 p.m. Wednesday at a Dallas hospital of complications from prostate cancer. He was 74.

Hunt's decision to relocate the Dallas Texans of the fledgling and struggling American Football League and rename them the Kansas City Chiefs in 1963 helped establish the region as a major-league community and ensured that big-time sports would continue here for generations to come.

His belief in Kansas City was rewarded by the club's appearance in two of the first four Super Bowls, with the Chiefs winning the NFL championship in 1970.

"He changed our way of life," said civic booster Bill Grigsby, a member of the Chiefs broadcast team since their arrival. "Despite the fact it was tough going in the beginning, he hung in there and has done so much for Kansas City."

"He has given the people here something to hang on to and enjoy. Our life would not be the same without that man."

Hunt was stricken with prostate cancer in September 1998 and underwent a series of chemotherapy treatments. In October 2003 he had surgery to remove the prostate gland.

"We are very grateful for the thoughts and prayers we have received over the last few weeks, and we ask that our privacy be respected in this difficult time," said Clark Hunt, one of Lamar Hunt's four children and Chiefs chairman of the board.

Hunt was one of the creators of the AFL in 1959 and was a principal negotiator in the merger of the AFL and NFL in 1966. He was credited with coining the term "Super Bowl" for what's turned out to be the country's most-watched sporting event, with the name coming from his children's toy "Super Ball."

Hunt also was a driving force in the creation of the Truman Sports Complex. The twin-stadium idea of Arrowhead Stadium, completed in 1972, and Royals Stadium in 1973 was years ahead of its time and later copied by other cities.

Fred Arbanas, a Chiefs Hall of Fame tight end and now a Jackson County legislator, not only played nine seasons for Hunt, but also worked with him on pushing through the stadium renovations. He said Hunt never lost his humble nature.

"He was a real gentleman and a tribute to the game," Arbanas said. "A lot of owners have been boisterous and arrogant. You never saw Lamar that way. All the trips we took on airplanes, Lamar would be helping serve food to the players, bringing them drinks and picking up the trash. He just pitched in. ..."

"He's not going to be forgotten. He's done too much for this community. The community has put out a lot of money for his football team, too, but he also took a big chance and spent a lot of money in this community."

Hunt not only made Arrowhead Stadium a showplace for NFL games, but also was at the forefront in bringing big-time college football to Kansas City. Arrowhead has been the site for 16 college games since 1972, including four Big 12 Conference championship games and several interconference matchups such as Kansas State-California and Florida State-Iowa State.

"In so many ways, Lamar Hunt made our city major league," said Kevin Gray, president of the Kansas City Sports Commission. "He took a gamble in bringing his team to Kansas City, and the overwhelming admiration that people have for him is remarkable.

"We take many things for granted, and we have been so blessed to have not only the finest owner in professional sports, but unquestionably one of the classiest individuals I have ever had the pleasure to know in this business."

Clark Hunt, 41, will oversee the family's sports interests.

Although Hunt never lived in Kansas City, he contributed significantly to the area's economy. Hunt, as chairman of Dallas-based Unity Hunt Inc., a large, diversified private company, also owned Hunt Midwest Enterprises, located within an underground business complex in Kansas City.

Hunt Midwest Enterprises developed two multimillion-dollar recreational theme parks in Kansas City -- Worlds of Fun and Oceans of Fun. Both parks were sold in 1995. Hunt Midwest also is the key corporation in the development of the Kansas City International Foreign Trade Zone and owns a limestone rock mining company.

Hunt, who was born in El Dorado, Ark., at one time was one of the world's richest men. His fortune, inherited from his father, H.L. Hunt, had its foundation in the oil business.

But unlike some who inherit wealth, Hunt carved out his own niche. He became one of the world's true sportsmen, changing the face of three professional sports in America through his founding of the American Football League in 1959, forming World Championship Tennis in 1967 and serving as a charter owner-operator of Major League Soccer in 1996.

Hunt also was a minority owner of the Chicago Bulls, two minor-league baseball teams in Dallas and Fort Worth, and at one time sought to purchase the Washington Senators baseball team and move them to Dallas. Later he made an offer for the Kansas City Royals.

But it was professional football where Hunt made his most lasting mark.

Hunt was married twice. His son, Lamar Jr., and daughter, Sharron, are children of his first marriage. He married Norma Lynn Knobel, who was an American history teacher at Richardson High School near Dallas, on Jan. 22, 1964. They have two sons, Clark and Daniel. He has 13 grandchildren.

» Quarterback Tyler Thigpen showed flashes with his arm and with his legs.

» The Chiefs drafted Dwayne Bowe with the hope he would be their go-to receiver.

Chapter 12
The End of the Carl Regime

As the dismal 2008 season was winding down, Clark Hunt made the announcement that Carl Peterson, the man who had resurrected a dying franchise, was out after 20 years directing the Chiefs.

Hunt called the move a mutual decision. Peterson, though, was not at the announcement.

"With our coaches coming into the last year of their contracts, he understood the right decision from an organizational standpoint was to make this change and announce it at this point," Hunt said. "He was very much in agreement.

"As our conversations continued, we both concluded that the right thing for the organization and the team was to break the ties completely. What gives us the best chance is the clean break we agreed upon."

Peterson said in a statement: "I am proud of my association with the Kansas City Chiefs and our many accomplishments over the last 20 years. I thank the Hunt family for the opportunity to lead the Chiefs organization and sincerely appreciate all the coaches, players, administrators and Chiefs employees with whom I've had the pleasure of working in my time here."

While the dreadful 2007 and 2008 seasons didn't help Peterson's cause, Hunt indicated that after 20 years it simply was time for the Chiefs to move on.

Hunt and Peterson discussed various scenarios that could have kept Peterson with the Chiefs, including one in which Peterson would have stayed as president but yielded control over the football side. As Hunt said, though, the decision was made that Peterson would step completely away.

Peterson left behind a varied legacy.

No one can dispute his efforts in turning the franchise around. He revived an entire city's passion for the Chiefs. His acquisitions of Joe Montana and Marcus Allen thrust the Chiefs into the national spotlight.

Peterson, though, fell short of his ultimate goal: Getting to and winning a Super Bowl.

"I have a tremendous amount of respect for Carl, and I have a tremendous amount of gratitude for what he's done for our family and the Chiefs' organization," Hunt said. "In some ways, it's like saying goodbye to a family member.

"Carl in a lot of ways has been a mentor for me in the time I've been around the Chiefs. I've learned quite a bit from him and know that I'll miss him."

At Last, Thomas Joins the Hall

The Kansas City Star | 2009

TAMPA, Fla. | When Derrick Thomas' name was announced for inclusion in the 2009 Pro Football Hall of Fame class, his mother screeched and the five-year wait for this moment turned inconsequential.

Derrick Thomas is a football immortal. His name is forever linked to Lawrence Taylor's and Dick Butkus' and Reggie White's and all the other all-time defensive greats. And now we know we watched, chronicled and celebrated a Hall of Famer.

D.T. to Canton is our Super Bowl run, the payoff for 20 years of dedication to Chiefs football.

Thomas rushed the quarterback when the league was in its transitional phase to the short, West Coast passing game. The style of attack was set up to eliminate the effect of speed rushers such as Thomas.

Thomas was a must-be-accounted-for force. He perfected the art of the tomahawk-strip sack. Every defensive player in the league chops at the football now when making a tackle. They're mimicking Derrick Thomas.

You know the numbers, the 126 ½ sacks, the seven-sack game, the forced fumble once every four games and the nine Pro Bowl appearances.

The numbers don't define Derrick Thomas. To appreciate Thomas, to fully understand his influence, you had to experience him on a regular basis. His personality gave the Chiefs a swagger they have never been able to replace. In that way, Thomas was like Baltimore middle linebacker Ray Lewis minus the pregame dance.

Thomas gave the Chiefs a chance to win every game. You never knew when he'd cause a turnover that would swing the contest.

A New Direction: The Pioli Way

In finding a replacement for Peterson, Hunt sought a man with a proven background. So, on Jan. 13, 2009, Hunt named Scott Pioli the fifth general manager in Chiefs history. Pioli had been serving as the vice president of player personnel for perhaps the top organization in all of football – the New England Patriots.

> *"The thing we're trying to build here is not just a team for 2009, not just for 2010," said Pioli, who helped New England to three Super Bowl championships in his nine seasons with the Patriots. "The goal is to build a team that consistently competes for championships, that has a long shelf life of being a good football team.*

» Chiefs coach Todd Haley, above left, is introduced to Kansas City by general manager Scott Pioli. Clark Hunt hopes to transform his father's vision into future Chiefs' success.

"The vision for this football team and the direction that we plan to head in is to build a football team. We built a football team in New England, and we'll build a football team here. My job is not to collect talent. It's to build a team. Individuals go to Pro Bowls. Teams win championships. That's our goal here."

One of Pioli's first tasks was to settle the coaching staff. He fired Herm Edwards and hired former Arizona offensive coordinator Todd Haley.

Haley, in his second season with the Cardinals, called the plays for an offense that reached the Super Bowl.

» Pioli promises to build the Chiefs in a similar manner to which the Patriots were built, focusing on the future, not just one season.

Pioli's reputation as one of the best talent evaluators in the game made Hunt's decision much easier.

"I was eager to get the best person, and at the end of the day Scott was head and shoulders above everyone else we talked to," Hunt said. "I went into the interview thinking there was no way that this individual could live up to the hype surrounding him. At the end of the interview, I was like, 'Wow.' Not only did he live up to it, he exceeded it."

Pioli acknowledged he has his work cut out for him. In terms of finding talent, it might even be a more difficult task than Peterson faced in 1989.

> *"There needs to be some changes on this football team," Pioli said. "With the way the team performed this year and what the record is, there needs to be changes. This is going to be a team that is certainly going into transition.*

"This is going to be a very methodical process in building this football team. We're going to start from the ground up and build a foundation and move ahead and touch every part of the football operation. The patience I know Clark has told me he's going to show is going to be rewarded."

>> *One of Pioli's first player moves was to bring in former Patriots quarterback Matt Cassel (7), who will be under the guidance of Haley (above).*

Chiefs Year by Year

Year	Record	Coach	Finish
1960 (Texans)	**8-6**	Hank Stram	2nd AFL West
1961 (Texans)	**6-8**	Hank Stram	2nd AFL West
1962 (Texans)	**11-3**	Hank Stram	1st AFL West
1963 (Chiefs)	**5-7-2**	Hank Stram	3rd AFL West
1964	**7-7**	Hank Stram	2nd AFL West
1965	**7-5-2**	Hank Stram	3rd AFL West
1966	**11-2-1**	Hank Stram	1st AFL West
1967	**9-5**	Hank Stram	2nd AFL West
1968	**12-2**	Hank Stram	1st AFL West
1969	**11-3**	Hank Stram	2nd AFL West
1970	**7-5-2**	Hank Stram	2nd AFC West
1971	**10-3-1**	Hank Stram	1st AFC West
1972	**8-6**	Hank Stram	2nd AFC West
1973	**7-5-2**	Hank Stram	2nd AFC West
1974	**5-9**	Hank Stram	3rd AFC West
1975	**5-9**	Paul Wiggin	3rd AFC West
1976	**5-9**	Paul Wiggin	4th AFC West
1977	**2-12**	Paul Wiggin	(1-6) 5th AFC West
		Tom Bettis	(1-6)
1978	**4-12**	Marv Levy	5th AFC West
1979	**7-9**	Marv Levy	5th AFC West
1980	**8-8**	Marv Levy	3rd AFC West
1981	**9-7**	Marv Levy	3rd AFC West
1982	**3-6**	Marv Levy	4th AFC West
1983	**6-10**	John Mackovic	4th AFC West
1984	**8-8**	John Mackovic	4th AFC West
1985	**6-10**	John Mackovic	5th AFC West
1986	**10-6**	John Mackovic	2nd AFC West
1987	**4-11**	Frank Gansz	5th AFC West

1988	4-11-1	Frank Gansz	5th AFC West
1989	8-7-1	Marty Schottenheimer	2nd AFC West
1990	11-5	Marty Schottenheimer	2nd AFC West
1991	10-6	Marty Schottenheimer	2nd AFC West
1992	10-6	Marty Schottenheimer	2nd AFC West
1993	11-5	Marty Schottenheimer	1st AFC West
1994	9-7	Marty Schottenheimer	2nd AFC West
1995	13-3	Marty Schottenheimer	1st AFC West
1996	9-7	Marty Schottenheimer	2nd AFC West
1997	13-3	Marty Schottenheimer	1st AFC West
1998	7-9	Marty Schottenheimer	4th AFC West
1999	9-7	Gunther Cunningham	2nd AFC West
2000	7-9	Gunther Cunningham	3rd AFC West
2001	6-10	Dick Vermeil	4th AFC West
2002	8-8	Dick Vermeil	4th AFC West
2003	13-3	Dick Vermeil	1st AFC West
2004	7-9	Dick Vermeil	3rd AFC West
2005	10-6	Dick Vermeil	2nd AFC West
2006	9-7	Herm Edwards	2nd AFC West
2007	4-12	Herm Edwards	3rd AFC West
2008	2-14	Herm Edwards	4th AFC West

A Team for Kansas City 1989-2009

Chiefs Hall of Fame

1970	Lamar Hunt, Founder
1971	Mack Lee Hill, Running Back
1972	Jerry Mays, Defensive Tackle
1973	Fred Arbanas, Tight End
1974	Johnny Robinson, Safety
1975	Chris Burford, Receiver
1976	E.J. Holub, Center/Linebacker
1977	Jim Tyrer, Offensive Tackle
1978	Mike Garrett, Running Back
1979	Len Dawson, Quarterback
1980	Bobby Bell, Linebacker
1981	Buck Buchanan, Defensive Tackle
1982	Otis Taylor, Wide Receiver
1983	No Induction
1984	Ed Budde, Guard
1985	Willie Lanier, Linebacker
1986	Emmitt Thomas, Cornerback
1987	Hank Stram, Coach
1988	Jerrel Wilson, Punter
1989	Ed Podolak, Running Back
1990	Jim Lynch, Linebacker
1991	Abner Haynes, Running Back
1992	Jan Stenerud, Kicker
1993	Sherrill Headrick, Linebacker
1994	Jack Rudnay, Center
1995	Curtis McClinton, Running Back
1996	Deron Cherry, Safety
1997	Dave Hill, Tackle
1998	Art Still, Defensive End
1999	Lloyd Burruss, Cornerback

and Retired Numbers

2000	Christian Okoye, Running Back
2001	Derrick Thomas, Linebacker
2002	John Alt, Tackle
2003	Gary Spani, Linebacker
2004	Joe Delaney, Running Back
2005	Jack Steadman, Vice Chairman of the Board
2006	Neil Smith, Defensive End
2007	Albert Lewis, Cornerback
2008	Curley Culp, Defensive Tackle
2009	Nick Lowery, Kicker

Retired Jersey Numbers

3	Jan Stenerud, Kicker
16	Len Dawson, Quarterback
18	Emmitt Thomas, Cornerback
28	Abner Haynes, Running Back
33	Stone Johnson, Running Back
36	Mack Lee Hill, Running Back
58	Derrick Thomas, Linebacker
63	Willie Lanier, Linebacker
78	Bobby Bell, Linebacker
86	Buck Buchanan, Defensive Tackle

All-time playoffs

Year	Round	W/L	Opponent	PF	PA
2006	Wild Card	L	@ Indianapolis Colts	8	23
2003	Division	L	Indianapolis Colts	31	38
1997	Division	L	Denver Broncos	10	14
1995	Division	L	Indianapolis Colts	7	10
1994	Wild Card	L	@ Miami Dolphins	17	27
1993	Wild Card	W	Pittsburgh Steelers	27	24
	Division	W	@ Houston Oilers	28	20
	Conf Champ	L	@ Buffalo Bills	13	30
1992	Wild Card	L	@ San Diego Chargers	0	17
1991	Wild Card	W	Los Angeles Raiders	10	6
	Division	L	@ Buffalo Bills	14	37
1990	Wild Card	L	@ Miami Dolphins	16	17
1986	Wild Card	L	@ New York Jets	15	35
1971	Division	L	Miami Dolphins	24	27
1969	Division	W	@ New York Jets	13	6
	Conf Champ	W	@ Oakland Raiders	17	7
	Super Bowl	W	Minnesota Vikings	23	7
1968	Division	L	@ Oakland Raiders	6	41
1966	Conf Champ	W	@ Buffalo Bills	31	7
	Super Bowl	L	Green Bay Packers	10	35
1962	Championship	W	@ Houston Oilers	20	17

176 | A Sea of Red